In the Spirit
of Adventure

A History of the Catholic
Guides of Ireland

BY

Clare Brophy

VERITAS

Published in 2009 by
Veritas Publications
7–8 Lower Abbey Street
Dublin 1, Ireland
Email publications@veritas.ie
Website www.veritas.ie

ISBN 978 1 84730 193 2

10 9 8 7 6 5 4 3 2 1

Unless otherwise specified, the photographs contained in the colour sections of this
book appear courtesy of: Aíne Nic Giolla Choille; Lensmen & Associates;
Frank Gavin Photography; Clancy Photography; Fotografia Felici; and Photostyle.
We have been unable to uncover the origin of the photograph of the bombing of
North Strand and the visit to Ireland by President John F. Kennedy.

Designed by Lir Mac Cárthaigh

Printed in the Republic of Ireland by Hudson Killeen, Dublin

Veritas books are printed on paper made from the wood pulp of managed forests.
For every tree felled, at least one tree is planted, thereby renewing natural resources.

CONTENTS

ACKNOWLEDGEMENTS

Before reading this history, it is important to note that at one time or another there were Guide companies in every diocese in Ireland. However, due to time constraints and the lack of available records it was impossible to include them all here.

The author wishes to express sincere thanks to all those who gave their time and support to this history project, in particular Carol Ewings, Cecilia Browne, Betty O'Donovan, Dolores Farnan, Martha McGrath and Catherine Lenihan. Many thanks to Ruth Kennedy and the Veritas team for their professional advice and direction. A special thank you to older members of the organisation for sharing their memories, in particular May McGrath, May Garvan, Sheila Redmond, Pat Walsh and Carmel Hutchin. Many thanks also to Mrs Maureen Walsh née Loftus and Mr Sean Loftus. For giving their time and kindness many thanks to Fr A.J. Gaughan and Fr Jim O'Sullivan. From Waterford many thanks to Siobhan McCarthy for her assistance with research; also Bríd Galvin, Paula Brackenbury and all those who attended the get-together at the Tower Hotel in Waterford. From Cork many thanks to Breda Healy, May Dowling and everyone I met there, with a special thank you to those who contributed invaluable material to the project. From Belfast many thanks to Marian Stewart, Maire McGrath, Peggy McGoran, Josephine Higgins and all those I met in St Paul's Community Centre. From Dublin many thanks to Maria Carroll, Mairead Quinn and Suzanne Mason. For their advice and support many thanks to the staff of the National Office, Laura Saunders, Alison O'Grady, Antoinette Hosback and Joe Murphy. Many thanks to Noelle Dowling, Dublin Diocesan Archives, for her assistance with research. Many thanks also to the staff of the James Joyce Library, UCD; the Gilbert Library, Pearse Street; the Central Catholic Library, Merrion Square; Rathmines Library; National Library of Ireland; and the National Archives. With thanks to Linda Scales for her professional handling of the legalities involved in this project. For their constant advice, support and encouragement many thanks to Pat Cooke, Mary Buckley, Ruth Devine and Michael and Margaret McLoughlin. Most especially, I would like to thank Fergus, Tim and Jack Brophy for their love and support throughout.

ABBREVIATIONS

CGI	Catholic Guides of Ireland
CBSI	Catholic Boy Scouts of Ireland
IGG	Irish Girl Guides
CIGA	Council of Irish Guiding Associations
SAI	Scout Association of Ireland
WAGGGS	World Association of Girl Guides and Girl Scouts
CSSC	Catholic Social Service Conference
WOSM	World Organisation of Scouting Movements
ICCG	International Catholic Conference of Guiding
UNESCO	United Nations Educational Scientific and Cultural Organisation
GGUK	Girlguiding United Kingdom
EEC	European Economic Community

INTRODUCTION

In the course of research for this history of the Catholic Guides of Ireland, I have undertaken a journey that has led me through the decades from 1928. As a consequence I have been afforded a unique insight into the lives of many girls and young women from twentieth-century Ireland to the present day.

Women and Society

It must have seemed to many women in the early 1920s that the new Free State held all kinds of possibilities. Since the end of world war one the women's movement had made great strides. In 1918 the suffrage groups in Dublin celebrated when Britain granted women over the age of thirty the right to vote. A procession of women from all sections of society marched to William Street courthouse to vote. They represented various women's bodies such as the Irish Women's Workers Union, the Irish Women's Franchise League and Cumann na mBan.[1] Women were further empowered when the 1922 constitution of the Irish Free State granted them equal rights as citizens.

The post civil war situation resulted in a jostling for positions of power by religious and political bodies. Initially the early actions of the Cumann na nGaedheal government suggested an unwillingness to give the Catholic church too much influence in the affairs of state. The last British home rule bill for Ireland in 1920 had provided that the senate of an Irish parliament should include four Catholic bishops as well as two Church of Ireland bishops; but the Cumann na nGaedheal government appointed no clerics to the senate of the Irish Free State.[2] They did, however, appoint four women including Jennie Wyse Power, a strong advocate of women's rights.[3] In her capacity as Senator, through the 1920s and into the 1930s she tried to prevent the passing into law of several bills that excluded women from public life and she supported the 1930 Illegitimate Children's Bill that allowed unmarried mothers to claim support from the fathers of their children. She quoted Abraham Lincoln: 'there never was a woman went astray but there was a man to help her'.[4]

The global economic crisis at the time contributed to the reasoning behind the exclusion of women from some areas of the workforce. Most women were engaged in farming or domestic service but in the 1930s there was a slight rise in the employment of women in light industries. The 1935 Conditions of Employment Bill provoked considerable protest from women's groups as it prohibited the employment of women in some areas and fixed the proportion of women to men.[5] The Irish Women's Workers Union led by Louie Bennett organised a protest meeting in Dublin in November of that year but the bill was passed, despite opposition from Kathleen Clarke and Jennie Wyse Power in the Senate. Speaking out against the bill Power stated:

There is one thing in connection with the earnings of girls. I think we may be sure that what they earn goes directly into the home. They do not drink or play 'house' with it. [6]

Whyte pin-points the late 1920s as a time when a Catholic social movement really began to take root in Ireland, coinciding with the formation of the Catholic Girl Guide organisation.[7] The strong patriarchal system involving church and state that emerged at that time not only limited female participation in public life but also in areas such as sport. An editorial in *The Irish Times* in May 1928 complained of female participation in sporting activities: 'many girls are devoting themselves to public sports which demands violent exertion and sometimes, it would seem, a notable scantiness in clothing …' At the Paris Olympics in 1924 two Irish women represented Ireland in tennis. Four years later one Irish female swimmer competed in Amsterdam. In 1932 the Irish Olympic team contained no women members.[8]

The Catholic Guides of Ireland

As an all-female association that catered for young girls, initially the role of the Catholic Girl Guides of Ireland was to support the Catholic church in areas of morality, education, faith and discipline. While it was never considered a movement that held sway in matters social or political the Guides were often used to bolster prevailing views in these areas. Occasionally their overt Catholicism allowed for some unexpected subversive actions that were neither noticed nor questioned. As time went on their relationship with the Catholic church waned in tandem with changes in Irish society.

Many significant events in history impacted on the organisation, such as the 1937 Constitution, World War II, Vatican II and the Good Friday Agreement of 1998. As a thirty-two-county organisation, their northern members and, in turn, the association as a whole were affected by events in Northern Ireland. Their influence on twentieth-century Ireland has been such that many people today can still recall the brown uniform of the past, an image the Catholic Guides find difficult to lose. Keeping pace with the rapid rate of modernity and competing with the various enticements on offer to young girls brought about by the Celtic Tiger presents a challenge for the organisation today. However, as their history shows, there is very little they cannot contend with.

This history begins with the foundation of the organisation and the dispute between the women founders and the Catholic church. Incorporating a Catholic ethos, through Guiding the women intended to provide a non-competitive, fun, informal and social forum in which girls could learn and express themselves. However, the Catholic church intended to dominate at board level, leaving the women little say in the direction of the Guide movement. The women resisted but the struggle for control of the

Catholic Girl Guides was won by the church and led to the organisation being administered by diocese.

The 1930s saw the Guide organisation establishing itself with a constitution and a programme of Guide activities in keeping with the times. In contrast, the 1940s, particularly the war years, saw the Girl Guides being given opportunities to participate in activities not normally allocated to them. This helped to build confidence and, despite a regime advocating a woman's life in the home, created a feeling of camaraderie amongst them that may have sown the seeds for the women's liberation movement of the next generation.

By the 1950s, the Guides had become a highly respected association, with Guide activities regularly reported in the newspapers and on radio. Testimony to this was the number of high-profile guests who attended the annual parents' day events. The 1950s were also a time when the girls performed a series of operatic extravaganzas requiring considerable organisational skills and not inconsiderable acting, singing and dancing talent. This gave them an outlet for their creativity.

In the 1960s, everything changed. Changes to the form of the Mass brought about by Vatican II caused widespread debate. The Church adapted to calls for a more liberal modern way of life, as indeed did Irish society as a whole. The Guides continued to play an important role in providing a forum for girls to socialise and take part in Guide activities. However, a more questioning and better-educated generation of girls began to infiltrate, resulting in a revision of the Guide programme. Calls for more intellectually challenging courses such as accountancy, astrology and geology demonstrate a departure from the more traditional courses based around life in the home. Camping and hiking were consistently amongst the girls' favourites, allowing them freedom from household duties and parental control.

The 1970s saw the organisation come together to form joint policies on areas such as training and it was acknowledged that nationalisation would help to strengthen the association and provide an opportunity for membership of the World Association of Girl Guides and Girl Scouts. However, attaining membership would prove to be a long, protracted process that would take almost thirty years to reach conclusion.

By the 1980s violence and unrest in Northern Ireland had escalated, making Guiding for Catholic girls there difficult. All over the country, Guides participated in many events designed to promote peace. The opening of dialogue between the political factions led to hopes for a peaceful outcome. The extraordinary negotiations involving membership of the World Association for Catholic Guides of Ireland members in the North reflected the political situation regarding border recognition and cultural identity. At one point, negotiations hung on the outcome of the Good Friday Agreement of 1998. There are few examples of a peripheral, non-political voluntary organisation such as the Catholic Guides of Ireland being affected by such an important and historic legislative document.

As Irish society continued to change, so did the relationship between the Catholic Guides of Ireland and the church. Increasingly, both bodies diverged from each other. This situation is attributable to each party and simply evolved, reflecting Irish life.

Through the 1990s, the Guides took part in many educational and charitable events at an international level, while at home the Celtic Tiger presented challenges. The economic boom had created a more affluent society in which girls were able to afford and choose from a wide selection of extracurricular interests in competition with Guide activities. However, an awareness of the demands of a modern society has prompted the Guides to once more adapt and continue to bring Guiding to girls and young women in the twenty-first century.

Therefore, in the spirit of Adventure, Fortitude, Readiness and Courage, this is their story.

Notes

1. Marie O'Neill, *From Parnell to De Valera, A Biography of Jennie Wyse Power 1858–1941* (Dublin, 1991) p. 108

2. J.H. Whyte, *Church and State in Modern Ireland 1923–1979* (Dublin, 1980) p. 34

3. Marie O'Neill, *From Parnell to De Valera, A Biography of Jennie Wyse Power 1858–1941* (Dublin, 1991) p. 146

4. Ibid., pp. 168–9

5. Myrtle Hill, *Women in Ireland: A Century of Change* (Belfast, 2003) pp. 100–1

6. Marie O'Neill, *From Parnell to De Valera, A Biography of Jennie Wyse Power 1858–1941* (Dublin, 1991) p. 173

7. J.H. Whyte, *Church and State in Modern Ireland 1923–1979* (Dublin, 1980) p. 35

8. Myrtle Hill, *Women in Ireland: A Century of Change* (Belfast, 2003) p. 102

CHAPTER I

FOUNDATIONS:

A GUIDE MOVEMENT FOR CATHOLIC GIRLS

1928–1939

Whatever the political issues and the political movements from Catholic Emancipation to the end of the 1930s, the attitude of the Church to these was characterised by one fundamental feature: vigorous opposition to ideas and organisations it could not control ...[1]

Growth of Youth Organisations

By the 1920s youth organisations for boys and girls were an established feature of society, not only in Ireland but also in the broader international context. In Britain the religious-based youth movement, the Boys' Brigade, was founded in 1883 and had a disciplined militaristic style. In Ireland the Catholic Boys' Brigade had been formed in March 1894 and by the turn of the century they had an estimated membership of seven hundred boys. The objectives of this organisation were stated to be:

To crush vice and evil habits amongst boys; to instruct them thoroughly in the Catholic doctrine; to prepare them for the worthy reception of the sacraments; to give them habits of obedience, discipline and self respect; reverence and love for ecclesiastical authority and our holy religion; to promote their moral, physical and temporal well being and to give them habits of strict sobriety.[2]

In Germany in the mid-1890s informal excursions to the countryside surrounding Berlin were organised for children who came from heavily industrialised parts of the city. These trips to the country were considered beneficial for their health. Through hiking and camping in the open air a strong sense of comradeship developed. The youth movement became immensely popular throughout Germany with boys and girls alike, although mixing of the sexes within the organisation was not encouraged. By 1901 it was formally known as Vandervogel.[3]

In America at the turn of the twentieth century, Ernest Thompson Seton, a naturalist, artist and writer, founded a youth group called the Woodcraft Indians and in 1902 he published a guidebook for boys called *The Birch Bark Roll.*[4]

Robert Baden-Powell, on returning to Britain from military service in South Africa, initially considered scouting for youths as an addition to the already developed Boys' Brigade. In 1907 he held an enormously successful camping convention at Brownsea Island and published his book *Scouting for Boys* (1908). Subsequently, the Baden Powell Boy Scouts became a popular worldwide secular scouting organisation. A company was established in Ireland in 1909. This inevitably led to the formation of a similar movement for girls known as the Girl Guides run by Agnes Baden Powell, sister of Robert. A company of the Baden Powell Girl Guides was established in Harold's Cross in Dublin in 1911.[5]

At that time Ireland was part of the United Kingdom. Following the treaty negotiations with Britain, Ireland became the Irish Free State. In 1922 the Girl Guides became the Irish Free State Girl Guides and in 1928 they underwent a change of name again to the Irish Girl Guides. Many people at that time associated the Irish Girl Guides with the former British regime and it was perceived as a Protestant and mostly middle-class association. In reaction to this a similar Guide organisation to cater for the needs of Catholic girls was founded in 1928 called Clanna Bhríde, which ultimately became known as the Catholic Girl Guides of Ireland.

In the 1920s, Girl Guide and Girl Scout organisations from various countries had come together to form the World Association of Girl Guides and Girl Scouts (WAGGGS). The object of the World Association was to promote unity of purpose and common understanding in the fundamental principles of the Girl Guide/Girl Scout movements throughout the world, and to encourage friendship among girls of all nations. Their aim was to provide girls and young women with opportunities for self-training in the development of character, responsible citizenship and service to the community.[6]

Birth of the Catholic Girl Guides of Ireland

In April 1923 the pro-treaty party Cumann na nGaedheal was launched at the Mansion House in Dublin and led by W.T. Cosgrave. Faced with the daunting task of bringing stability to a country divided by civil war, the government sought advice on a variety of matters from the Catholic church. Both church and state believed 'it was imperative to ensure that boys and young men should no longer join political or militaristic organisations and that it was necessary to provide alternative organisations for young people'.[7] Fr Ernest Farrell was instrumental in forming the Catholic Boy Scouts of Ireland and ultimately the Catholic Girl Guides. He served as a curate in Greystones, Co. Wicklow from 1924 to 1927. While there he formed a Boys' Club that engaged in activities such as hiking and camping. He studied scouting from the handbook of the Boy Scouts of America and campaigned through the letters page of *Our Boys*, a popular youth magazine, for the establishment of a uniquely Catholic scouting organisation. With the support of his brother, Fr Thomas Farrell, and members of the influential Catholic lay organisation, the Knights of Columbanus, they sought to establish an Irish national scouting organisation with the backing of the church.[8] The Farrells drafted a constitution based on documentation from the Boy Scouts of America and in October 1926 the Catholic hierarchy approved of the establishment of the Catholic Boy Scouts of Ireland (CBSI). An organising council was appointed with Fr Thomas Farrell as secretary.[9]

CBSI became a great success and immediately plans were in place to form an organisation for girls. Clanna Bhríde had been formed in 1928 to provide a uniquely Irish style of Guiding for Catholic girls. By 1930, as numbers grew, a more formal administrative system was required, including a change of name, and once again Fr Thomas Farrell approached the Catholic hierarchy seeking backing and support.

The original organising committee for the proposed Catholic Girl Guides of Ireland came together through the Legion of Mary in Dublin. Margaret Loftus and Bridget Ward were both members of Our Lady Seat of Wisdom Praesidium of the Legion of Mary in Newman House, St Stephen's Green, Dublin. Ward was described as 'a very spiritual person, gentle and unassuming and humble about the great work she was doing with the aid of a few lay helpers'.[10] Margaret Loftus had trained as a Domestic Science teacher and taught in impoverished areas of Dublin city. She witnessed first-hand the dreadful living conditions of some girls and young women. She was approached by her friend, Frank Duff, founder of the Legion of Mary, and asked to help form a girl guide movement.[11] From the outset Brigid Ward was appointed National Secretary of the organisation with Margaret Loftus as President.[12]

One of the first commissioners for CBSI was Ernest Cullen, whose wife, along with Margaret Loftus and Bridget Ward, was one of the eleven original members cited by Fr Farrell as suitable to be on the organising committee. Many of the women are referenced in relation to their husband's occupation: for example, Mrs Margaret Loftus (wife of Dr. J.J. Loftus), Mrs Montgomery (wife of Film Censor).[13] Also included on the committee was the wife of P.J. Little, a Fianna Fáil TD and former editor of the Sinn Féin paper, *New Ireland*, and Louise Gavan Duffy, who had served in the GPO in 1916. She later founded Scoil Bhríde, an Irish-language secondary school for girls in Dublin.[14]

In a letter dated 7 June 1930 Fr Thomas Farrell wrote to the Archbishop of Dublin to assure him of the suitability of the committee:

> The members of the committee are women of education and of good social position. They are animated with the idea of using the Guide Movement developed on truly Catholic lines, to help our girls to attain to the high ideals of Catholic womanhood. They realise the pressing necessity there is for organised Catholic Action among our young girls and are prepared to work ardently for the ends aimed at in the proposed Catholic Girl Guide organisation.[15]

At that time, the church was concerned with what it saw as declining morality in Irish society.[16] In the 1920s and 1930s Catholic Action was composed of a number of pressure groups such as the Catholic Truth Society and the Irish Vigilence Association, who lobbied the government to put in place legislation on issues such as divorce and censorship.[17] Fr R.S. Devane, a Jesuit social worker, and laymen such as Frank Duff, founder of the Legion of Mary, worked to highlight moral and social problems such as the loss of parental control over young girls and the influence of 'obscene' newspapers and literature.[18] Another purpose of the Catholic Action body was to strengthen the Catholic faith, a sentiment expressed in a separate statement addressed to the Archbishop by the women organisers:

> There is in Ireland a branch of an English organisation known as the Girl Guide Association. In name this branch is non-sectarian. In fact it is Protestant. Just as scouting attracts boys, so guiding has a like attraction for girls, with the result that our Catholic girls are becoming members of this Protestant organisation. For some time past the activities of this organisation have greatly increased, serious efforts being made to induce our girls to join. Since the establishment of the Catholic Boy Scouts, the minds of the girls have been more strongly directed to the benefits afforded by Guiding.[19]

In Ireland an overall anti-Protestant sentiment prevailed. For example, in the same year, 1930, controversy surrounded the appointment of Letitia Dunbar-Harrison, a Trinity graduate, to the position of Mayo County Librarian on the grounds that she was Protestant. Mayo County Council refused to confirm her appointment, which resulted in the Gumman nGaedheal government stepping in to uphold the appointment. The government's actions are considered to have contributed to a decline in its popularity in favour of Fianna Fáil.[20]

A Synopsis of Policy for the Catholic Girl Guides of Ireland was prepared by the organising committee that reflected a uniquely Catholic, Irish ethos in contrast to the perceived 'Protestant, English' Guiding association. In September 1930 Fr Thomas Farrell sent a copy to each of the archbishops and bishops seeking support for the organisation, the aims of which are laid out as follows:

> to promote the methods, principles and exercises of Guiding among the Catholic girls of Ireland, to apply these methods, principles and exercises according to Catholic Irish ideals so as to help them to realise the ideals of womanhood, as a preparation for their responsibilities in the home and service for the community. In a higher conception, to elevate the present life of the girl, and so prepare her for the life to come.[21]

The policy and aims of the organisation were laid out in three Articles:

1. The Association is not to take the place of the religious sodalities, or in any way to be detrimental to their success, but shall encourage girls to become members of such organisations as a means of becoming better Guides.

2. The Association is absolutely non-political. Guides, when in uniform, shall not take part in any political activity, and they shall not discuss politics during Guide exercises.

3. The Association is Irish in outlook, and shall encourage girls to study the language, history, music and games of their country and to help in all that appertains to the revival of its Gaelic culture.

It was proposed by the committee that the association be organised as follows:

The Organisation proposes to work through Diocesan Councils and Local Associations, consisting of a President, Chaplain, Commissioners, Secretary etc. The supreme authority of the movement lies with the National Council, on which the Diocesan Councils and Local Associations have representation.[22]

The motto of the Guides was *Bí Ullamh* (be prepared). It was considered that in order for girls to live up to their motto they would need to be trained in all 'womanly occupations'.[23] Merit badges were awarded for proficiency in cooking, needlework, laundry, nursing and similar subjects. Girls were encouraged to take an interest in natural history and all forms of art. Most important of all was the merit badge for liturgy: every Girl Guide was expected to obtain this. Also of importance were the Irish speaker's and homemaker's badges, which together with the liturgy badge were given the distinction of being the only badges worn on the right arm. 'A girl winning these three badges becomes a National Guide – the Ideal Irishwoman.'[24]

In July 1932 an 'impressive ceremony took place at the Esplanade, Collins Barracks in Dublin'. It was the Flag Blessing of St Daire's Troop of Girl Guides in St Paul's parish. According to Fr Farrell, 'this was the first occasion on which they had the pleasure of having a Troop Colour of their Association blessed'. The *Irish Independent* reported that:

> The Girl Guide movement was intended to perpetuate the glorious tradition handed down to them by the womanhood of the past. The Association of Girl Guides held great promise for the future; it was mighty in its prospects and had behind it the glorious traditions of a faithful Irish womanhood.[25]

Fr Farrell paid tribute to the founders 'who in past years had ploughed the lonely furrow, who had worked to establish the organisation and had brought it to its present state of efficiency'.[26]

Friction between the Church and Women Founders

By 1933 the organising committee of the Catholic Girl Guides was preparing its constitution, similar to that of the Catholic Boy Scouts. However, early in 1933, Fr Thomas Farrell expressed concerns regarding the wording of the Guide promise: 'there is a tendency to make the natural aspect of the organisation over-shadow the Catholic aspect, and that is why I suggested that the Guide and Scout Promise should be the same'.[27] Relations between the Farrell brothers and the organising committee began to deteriorate when the women began to complain about the extent of clerical control over them. A meeting was held on Monday, 22 May 1933 to attempt to resolve differences. At that meeting Fr Ernest Farrell proposed that the following be inserted into the Catholic Girl Guide constitution:

> The Parish Priest of the parish or the local superior of a men's Religious House is the Controlling Authority within the Constitution of Companies within his parish or Religious House respectively, with power to delegate this authority to any Chaplain whom either may wish to appoint.[28]

This contradicted the committee's proposals in the original Synopsis of Policy sent to the bishops and archbishops outlined above, in which it was stated that the National Council of the Guide organisation would have supreme authority. After an open discussion the motion for inclusion in the constitution was lost by a decisive 11 votes to 4. The majority of women felt that it would be impossible to function effectively if 'they had no authority on any matter. It was felt that the chaplain's personal influence would always be such that even in matters outside the moral and religious, he would be paramount'.[29] He ignored the outcome of the vote by the Executive Council and called a 'secret meeting of captains' where he stated that the present Executive Council would not work under ecclesiastical authority. Feeling much maligned the Executive Committee considered his action unconstitutional.[30]

At that 'secret meeting' Fr Ernest Farrell formed a new organising committee from the captains of the Girl Guide companies. Despite requests from the original committee for Archbishop Edward Byrne to adjudicate on the actions of Fr Farrell, the Archbishop sanctioned a new committee devoted to clerical control. In December 1933 the captains wrote to the Archbishop stating:

> We have freely and definitely disassociated ourselves from any control exercised by Mrs Loftus and those associated with her and now look for direction only to the Chaplains and the new Organising Committee set up by them.[31]

Writing on the same day to the Archbishop, Margaret Loftus stated:

> We regret that our chaplains should have felt that they had a grievance as we have always stressed that our organisation was first Catholic. We believed that in a Girls' movement, to be successful it was necessary that each company should function under a local association consisting of representative ladies who, together with the chaplain, would be the controlling authority. As regards the Chaplain's position, it was felt that his personal influence as a priest gave him a sufficiently controlling power, leaving at the same time room for the initiative and interest of the other members of the local association.[32]

Despite repeated pleas by the women founders to Archbishop Edward Byrne to carry out an enquiry into the circumstances surrounding the case, by April 1934 the dispute had taken a turn for the worse. Bitterly the women recounted to the Archbishop that rumours that they were anti-clerical, ultra-national and extremist were being circulated and they requested an Ecclesiastical Court be set up to investigate events since May 1933. They claimed they were 'victims of a very grave injustice' and the only other means left to them would be to take the matter to a Civil Court, 'exposing the whole unsavoury matter'. They said that all their offers of peace had been ignored and in a despairing tone stated:

It is not necessary for us to point out the evil results which would follow generally upon the eventual success of this manoeuvre to put aside rightful authority. If the lay people were made to feel that priests desirous of more power had only to do as has been done in our case (i.e. allege anti-clericalism, organise secretly and illegally) to throw down the constitutionally established order in all places, they would proceed to safeguard themselves and to look doubtfully upon every action of the priest. In this lies the beginning of real anti-clericalism. Unfortunately, this sad affair is now widely known and spoken of; every centre where a company of self-constituted Guides exists is a seething pot of calumny against us, casting the gravest reflection on each individual member of our Council. We want to assure Your Grace of our absolute loyalty whilst taking any steps that may be deemed necessary to publicly (if needs be) defend our character, and to strenuously oppose every effort of Fr Farrell to use the mighty power of the church unjustly to take possession of the Organisation which we founded, and for whose ideals we have worked for over seven years.[33]

This letter shows the courageous nature of the women. They were ignored and the church took control of the Guide organisation. In a revealing handwritten letter dated July 1934, Fr Thomas Farrell, writing to an unnamed Monsignor, outlined his views concerning the constitution of the Guiding organisation:

> from the point of ecclesiastical control this constitution is altogether unsatisfactory. A large number of amendments and additions are required so as to make the organisation safe from being dominated by lay control ... I respectfully suggest there should be a rule in the approved constitution declaring that fundamental rules of the constitution are subject to review and alteration only by the Bishops.[34]

He concluded with this statement:

> The interest of the Chaplains in the Guide organisation lies chiefly in the fact that the organisation being established and promoted as a Catholic Action body has a purpose and an end entirely spiritual and supernatural (the ordinary Guide activities are used as an attraction and as a means of recreation).[35]

As far as the women organisers were concerned, the objective of the Guide movement was to improve the lives of young girls whilst embracing a Catholic ethos. They considered that the extent of clerical control imposed on the organisation would render them powerless in making any decisions regarding the direction of the movement. Fr Thomas Farrell intended the Guide organisation to act as another pressure group under the umbrella of Catholic Action.

In a letter dated 22 November 1934, Archbishop Byrne wrote to Margaret Loftus. She had requested a 'peaceful joining of the ranks of the Guides'.[36] Byrne was pleased with these signs of reconciliation and expressed the hope that Margaret Loftus and the other committee members could meet with the chaplains and the leaders of the Dublin Companies, put aside their differences and form a National and Executive Council to manage the organisation. But Byrne warned:

> Should the hopes for peace which I have placed in the holding of a National Council be frustrated, I will feel obliged to put an end to the present deplorable situation by withdrawing my approval from all existing bodies of the Guide movement in my diocese and seriously considering the establishment on a purely diocesan basis of an entirely independent Catholic Girl Guide organisation for Dublin.[37]

A resolution could not be found and in 1935 the Catholic Girl Guides were organised and administered by diocese. Margaret Loftus and Bridget Ward refused to let the matter rest. Through the then Papal Nuncio (diplomatic representative of the Pope), Most Rev. Dr Robinson, the women forwarded a detailed account of the dispute to Pope Pius XI in Rome. Subsequently, in October 1935, they were invited to meet with Monsignor Bearzotti at the Nunciature in Dublin where he read to them an

English translation of a letter written in Italian by the Pope's Secretary.

> With regard to what Mrs Margaret Loftus and Mrs Bridget Ward put before the Holy Father in documents forwarded to him, the answer is plain from instructions issued repeatedly by the Holy See in the matter of Catholic Action. The Holy See desires that any societies helping in Catholic Action should be subject to the Bishop and should help him in perfect filial obedience.
>
> No doubt it is entertained that the two good ladies referred to who have worked so hard and so zealously for the welfare of girls will, even though it means giving up their personal views now, be quite ready to set an example of whole-hearted and generous discipline, and show by their actions their complete submission to the Holy See.[38]

Having no options left open to them, the women acknowledged the letter from the Pope's Secretary thanking him for his kind words in regard to their work for the welfare of girls and assured him that they would submit to the wishes of the Holy Father. At the meeting's conclusion, Monsignor Bearzotti suggested they visit Archbishop Byrne. They explained that he had ignored several requests from them for an interview. Monsignor Bearzotti said that he would arrange it. Margaret Loftus and Bridget Ward hoped 'that even at the eleventh hour

His Grace might give us some measure of justice'.[39] However, before the interview, owing to the poor health of the Archbishop, they were asked not to touch on any contentious matters. 'So while His Grace was very courteous, talking with us for a considerable time, and giving us his blessing on our departure, the interview was abortive of any good to us.'[40]

Margaret Loftus, Bridget Ward and others on the committee took a brave stand to try to maintain control of an organisation they had helped build. However, church authority proved too strong and the women were effectively sidelined from the organisation.

The original committee of the Catholic Girl Guides headed by Margaret Loftus and Bridget Ward had been administered from an office at 50 Middle Abbey Street in Dublin. The split within the organisation became official when in August 1936 a lease was signed by the Dublin United Tramways Company and the new committee for the Guides represented by Fr Michael Clarke and Fr Thomas Farrell on an office located at Dawson Street in Dublin at a yearly rent of £50 inclusive.[41]

Administered by Diocese

Now firmly under the control of the church, the Catholic Guides spread throughout Ireland. Originally founded as a National Association it was decided by Archbishop Byrne that the Catholic Guides now be administered by diocese. As laid out in the 1936 Constitution, the organisation was dominated by a Diocesan Council whose duty it was to elect the Executive Committee. The Council consisted of a Diocesan Chaplain, Diocesan Commissioner, Assistant Diocesan Commissioner, District Captains, Chaplains and Captains. The archbishop of the diocese was Chairman of the Council and in his absence the Diocesan Chaplain had the right of a casting vote. The Executive Committee consisted of the Diocesan Chaplain, two other chaplains and three lay members as selected by the Diocesan Council. One of the chaplains on the Executive Committee would act as Honorary Treasurer, having responsibility for all monies. In Article 4 Section 2, the role of the Diocesan Chaplain was laid out as follows:

> The Archbishop appoints the Diocesan Chaplain. The Diocesan Chaplain is, under the Archbishop, the controlling authority in all matters pertaining to the maintenance, development and general welfare of the Organisation in the Diocese, and all acts of the Diocesan Council or the Executive Committee are to be construed having regard to this rule.[42]

The new administration applied to each diocese where there were Catholic Girl Guides and, regardless of the controversy regarding control of the organisation, Guiding had spread through clerical routes throughout Ireland.

Guide Companies

Throughout the organisation, Guide companies were organised along similar lines. At company meetings, 'corners' was the term for study where each Guide would retire to study for her merit badges. Each meeting concluded with the singing of the Guide anthem. Companies were divided into different groups or patrols with titles such as Skylarks, Robins and Thrushes, and each group was assigned a patrol leader. Registering new members was the role of the captain of the company. Membership cards were completed for each enrolled member and included the date the Guide joined, the date of enrolment, the tests completed and badges awarded. A yearly registration fee was paid by each Guide to cover expenses such as books and equipment. This fee reflected the ability of the Guide to pay. Each company looked after their own funds. Fundraising events such as concerts, raffles and craft sales helped to subsidise the purchase of uniforms, camping trips, outings and insurance.[43]

The Catholic Girl Guides of Ireland was a thirty-two county organisation regardless of the political boundary that separated the six counties in Northern Ireland. A Catholic Guiding movement had been formed in 1932 in St Peter's Pro-Cathedral, Belfast, in the Diocese of Down and Connor. By the late 1930s in the North of Ireland, Guide companies had been formed in Mount Carmel, Kilkeel and Downpatrick, Co. Down, and areas of Belfast such as College Square North and St Michael's. There were many letters to Dublin requesting uniforms, badges and information on company colours and patrol emblems, which suggests the organisation there had a large membership and was growing.

Bridie O'Rourke, who later became Sr Francis Joan, is attributed with bringing Guiding to Waterford. She, along with the nuns at the Sisters of Charity Convent in Lady Lane, Waterford City, established St Attracta's Catholic Girl Guide Company in October 1932 in the Diocese of Waterford and Lismore. Another nun, Sr Rose, later set up a training company in the convent for the purpose of training leaders. As a result of these actions, Guiding soon spread to all areas of Waterford.

In the same year, 1932, in Cork city the Catholic Guides were established with the help of Monsignor John Bastible; Rose Lynch became the first Diocesan Commissioner in the Diocese of Cork and Ross. Backed by the Bishop of Cork, Dr Cohalan, and with the help of Guides from Killarney, Rose Lynch founded five companies with girls recruited from local schools. In 1934 in Cork, Lynch purchased four railway carriages for £5 each and set them up in a field in Redbarn, Youghal. One car was used as the dining area and the other three for sleeping. Blankets were folded on the beds in a particular way to allow two to sleep head to toe. This became the location for many summer camps for Cork Girl Guides up until 1964.[44] In 1934 the *Cork Examiner* reported:

It is a marvellous place for a holiday. The Guides have their own field of games and a few yards away is the splendid stretch of strand on which all sorts of games and competitions may be enjoyed. The bathing is excellent and very safe and a special bathing shelter has been erected near the camp in the field over looking [sic] the beach.[45]

But if there's going to be a life hereafter
As every Girl Guide knows there is going to be
I will ask my Lord to let me make my heaven
In that little Camp beside the Irish Sea.[46]

Through the 1930s visits were often exchanged between Cork and Dublin Guides. On a trip to Dublin in 1933, Cork Guides were given a tour of Dublin with refreshments and entertainment laid on at the Winter Garden, adjacent to the Theatre Royal.[47] In July 1934 a number of Dublin Girl Guides travelled to Cork, where the Cork Guides played host and brought them on a sight-seeing tour of Cork. This included a trip on a steamer to Cobh, where they visited St Colman's Cathedral.[48]

In Dublin, Guide companies were cropping up in areas all around the city and it was soon apparent that the premises at Dawson Street was too small for the administration of the growing Guide organisation. A suitable headquarters was identified as 36/37 Harrington Street, two Georgian houses knocked into one – originally a Methodist female orphan school. The total cost of purchasing the property came to £2,450. A mortgage of £2,000 was taken out by a Committee of Trustees on behalf of the Dublin Diocese and the balance was donated. Arthur O'Hagan & Son Solicitors handled the transaction and the deal was closed in July 1937.[49] As numbers in Dublin began to grow steadily the need for a hall to hold events and fundraisers became obvious and Archbishop Byrne gave permission for the land at the back of Harrington Street headquarters to be used as the site for the hall. Building Contractors Smith & Pearson Ltd quoted £6,000 for the cost of building the hall and, despite the outbreak of war and the short supply of building materials, work went ahead.[50]

Role of Women

To appreciate some of the activities the Guides took part in, it may be beneficial to reflect on the role of girls and women in Irish society at the time the Catholic Girl Guide Organisation was founded. Many Catholic periodicals and pastoral letters of the time advocated women's life in the home. In 1934 Dr Dignan, Bishop of Clonfert, in his pastoral letter recommended that 'because girls' natural place is in the home, mothers should instruct them in housekeeping'. Writing in the *Irish Messenger* in 1937, Fr Stephen J. Browne believed that employment of daughters outside the home was interfering with home life.[51] Therefore, as can be seen from the diary of Betty Casey, a Guide in Cork in 1932,

Guide activities such as tracking coincided with merit badge awards for excellence in activities based around life in the home.

In Italy in the 1930s, with the encouragement of the papacy, women's participation in the workforce was also discouraged.[52] *The Italian Youth of Catholic Action (Girls)* was founded in 1918 in Milan by Pope Benedict XV and spread rapidly throughout Italy. In their literature they stated 'at home they bring life and impulse to the Housewives Movement to unite all the youth of that section'.[53]

It is probable, however, that there were more mundane economic reasons that contributed to the ideology of women as homemakers. In Britain and Germany the war had provided new opportunities for women. However, many of the traditionally male-dominated jobs women had taken on during the war were closed to them afterwards when men returned to the workforce.[54] Later, due to the global economic depression following the 1929 Wall Street Crash, women were actively discouraged from participating in the workforce. With the establishment of the Irish Free State, the Free State Constitution (1922) provided the same rights concerning citizenship for women as it did for men – the right to vote. Many women believed that ultimately this would extend to equality in the workplace. However, even the feminist female trade unionist, Louie Bennett, questioned the usefulness of women working at all as it had 'not raised standards of living, was a menace to family life and blocked the employment of men'.[55]

Guide Activities

Although many Guide activities focussed on the home, there were also those that gave girls an opportunity to escape school and household chores. Hiking was a favourite activity of many guides. Sunday 10 July 1932 was May McGrath's first hike with Buidean Eidín to Donabate: 'we tramped through fields, gates and over stiles until we reached the strand to be met with a gloriously refreshing sea breeze'.[56] Some of the girls went swimming while others collected firewood for a fire to boil kettles for tea. Games such as chasing, follow-the-leader and charades were played, while exercises in tracking, signalling and knots were practised. Another hike in September was organised to Ballycorus near Bray, Co. Wicklow, where the company had tea beside the lead mines chimney.

As can be seen from the diaries of Betty Casey and May McGrath, the

A Hike

girls took great pride in taking care of their logbooks and much attention centred on presentation. The considerable artistic rendering given to poems in May McGrath's logbook, suggests a great love of both poetry and art.

At the time, Guiding provided many activities not catered for in schools. May recalled that company drill was taught by a Miss McCormack and included marching in formation in a series of complex manoeuvres. Semaphore practice included signalling, and the sending and receiving of messages including Morse code. [57] In Dublin the Guides performed at an annual Grand Rally that allowed the girls to show off their talents. The fourth Grand Rally on 18 November 1934 organised by the Guides in the Diocese of Dublin was held in the Olympia Theatre and included a variety of performances including a pageant, Irish dancing, recitation, folk dancing and drill.

A similar annual event was held in Cork. In 1936 a fête and exhibition was held at the Arcadia Ballroom where it was reported:

> There was a large attendance of clergy and laity when the Cork branch of the Catholic Girl Guides of Ireland held a féte and exhibition of Guide craft at which his Lordship the Bishop of Cork, Most Rev. Dr Cohalan was present.[58]

At the conclusion of the event, Monsignor Sexton stated:

> It is a most necessary movement ... because today we want women who are leaders in the march of the nation.[59]

Céilís were also a feature of the fêtes in Cork, with the Pat Crowley Band providing the music for an evening of dancing from 8 p.m. to midnight.

Opportunities for Travel

Pilgrimages presented opportunities for Guides to travel and see the world. In 1934 Rose Lynch from Cork and Pauline Murray, Assistant Commissioner of the Guides in the Dublin Diocese, led a pilgrimage to Rome in which Guides from all over Ireland took part. The journey took them through London, Paris, Turin and Genoa. They stayed at the Instituto Mater Amabilis Convent in Rome. One of the highlights of the pilgrimage was the canonisation in St Peter's Square of Don Bosco on 1 April 1934.[60] The Guides were entertained by students of the Irish College in Rome, and the trip was widely reported in Irish newspapers – the *Irish Press* ran an article under the headline 'High Privilege for Irish Guides':

> One hundred and nine members of the Catholic Girl Guides of Ireland in uniform, from Dublin, Cork, Waterford, Westport, Tipperary and Clare,

who left Dublin last night for Rome will be on first aid duty in St Peter's on Sunday during the ceremony of the Canonisation of Blessed John Bosco.[61]

On the 5 April 1934 the Guides were granted an audience with Pope Pius XI, where they presented him with an address written in Italian, mounted on vellum and beautifully decorated with a Celtic design. It stated:

> Our Guide movement although young embraces over 2,000 Catholic Irish girls … Our aims are to love and serve God and our holy church; to help our neighbours always and, while adhering strictly to the wishes expressed by your Holiness with regard to girls' physical activities, to fit ourselves both spiritually and physically to make the Catholic Girl Guides of Ireland a stronghold of Catholic Action in our dear country.[62]

In response the Pope thanked the Guides for their expressions of devotion and commended them on their 'Fortitude, Readiness and Courage' in the propagation of the faith, inspiring the Guides to adopt the terms as their motto.

In a letter to her aunt, Betty Casey, who was fifteen years old in 1934, recalled another trip to a convent in Bruges, Belgium, organised by the Guides in July of that year.[63] At that time travel was difficult and it often took several days to reach a destination. The object of the trip was to take part in a series of up-to-date Guide training exercises practiced by the Belgium Guides. The journey took two days with a stopover in London, where Betty went sightseeing. There she met up with Guides from Dublin, Waterford and Westport, Co. Mayo, and they all continued on their journey. They stayed at the historic Convent of the Sacred Heart of the Retreat, situated on the site of the Palace of Marie of Burgundy.[64] When they arrived she recalled:

> We did not do much the first day, just walking around Bruges. In the morning we had drill and the Commissioner from Brussels and another Captain came. With them we went tracking in a wood in the evening. We had tea there too. Dinner was at 6.45pm. Then we usually had a sing-song, games or a camp-fire before bed. On Tuesday we went by special bus to Zeebrugge where there is a lovely strand. Some of us visited the Museum there, full of relics of the war. We also had a ride on a horse on the strand and went paddling.[65]

The experience of foreign travel for most people in Ireland in the 1930s would have been rare. Through Guiding these girls were presented with the opportunity of seeing other countries, experiencing other cultures and broadening their education generally.

Eucharistic Congress

In many ways Catholicism was central to Irish nationalist ideology. In 1931 Pope Pius XI issued the encyclical *Quadragesimo Anno*, which advocated social reforms and a 'general moral revival'.[66] When Eamon de Valera came to power in 1932 an advertisement was issued stating that the Fianna Fáil party would govern 'in accordance with the principles enunciated in the encyclicals of Pope Pius XI on social order'.[67] In an address to the Papal Legate at St Patrick's Hall, Dublin Castle, which was attended by distinguished churchmen and laymen, he equated 'Irish' with 'Catholic' and made it clear that he considered Ireland to be an essentially Catholic nation.[68] This had a lot to do with consolidating Ireland's identity distinct from Britain.

The Eucharistic Congress in June 1932 was an example of the collaboration between church and state, with de Valera making many public appearances in the company of Irish bishops. The Eucharistic Congress required the mass involvement of church, state and citizens on a grand scale. It was estimated that in Dublin there were twelve miles of bunting and that at least one million people participated in the event, including hundreds of Catholic Girl Guides.[69]

Guides from St Colman's in the North of Ireland travelled to Dublin for the Congress and were photographed outside the Theatre Royal, Hippodrome and Winter Garden, situated close to Trinity College in Dublin.

Preparation for the Congress had been ongoing for weeks prior to the event. Schools located near Congress events were closed and used as hostels.[70] To assist with stewarding, some of the girls were given basic lessons in first aid. In her diary May McGrath wrote:

> As we did not feel proficient enough in first aid work we were given the duty of carrying water bottles. From the time of our arrival in the park at 10 a.m. we were kept busy until 6 p.m. The children seemed to have an unquenchable thirst and we began to fear that the huge supply of water would run out. We felt that if we gave water in abundance to the people in our section, there would be little need of first aid. Despite this, however, we were obliged to attend to numerous fainting cases. It was a wearying day but we remembered our Guide Laws and refrained from even the slightest grumble. Remembering instructions, we left the trams for our elders and walked home *very slowly* not knowing whether we were glad or sorry that our work was finished.[71]

An international Camp for Guides and Scouts attending the Congress was held in Powerscourt Park in Enniskerry, Co. Wicklow. Guides from around the world including a large contingent of Dutch Girl Guides made camp there for the duration of the Congress. Closer to home, the *Cork Examiner* reported that 'a large number of Girl Guides left for Dublin by the 11.40 a.m. train. They will hold camp in Powerscourt Park during the Congress and will attend the ceremonies in Dublin'.[72] In Cork itself, the Guides formally attended the Eucharistic Congress open air mass at the Mardyke.

Leadership

The recruitment and training of suitable leaders for the organisation was always challenging. Fr Michael Clarke who was Chaplain to the Dublin Guides in the 1930s stated:

> The girls we require ... are from 20 to 30 years of age, if possible of secondary school education, and sufficiently interested in this branch of Catholic Action, to devote to it at least two nights a week.[73]

Clarke did not want to approach other organisations within Catholic Action for help with recruitment of leaders, such as the Legion of Mary, as that would deplete their members. Approaches therefore were made to the Catholic Women's Federation of Secondary School Unions to see if past pupils would be interested in getting involved in Guiding. It was mostly through the schools or religious orders that leaders came forward. Peggy Byrne from Ringsend wrote to Fr Clarke in 1939 having been recommended by Sr Brendan of the Convent of Mercy in Arklow:

Here in Ringsend we have a big parish, there are clubs and a Boy Scout Company for the boys, but so far there is nothing for the girls. If you could let me have the required information I could talk to our P.P. Fr Neary about it. Sr Brendan tells me your biggest difficulty is finding girls to train for Captains, I would be willing to take the course, I am 21 years of age, but I have not Secondary education, if however, you feel I would be acceptable, I am very interested and would do my best to make it a success.

Yours Sincerely
Peggy Byrne.[74]

Peggy's lack of secondary level education was not unusual for the time. In a report on Religious Examination of Primary Schools in the Diocese of Dublin in 1937 it was found that the average school-leaving age for girls was fourteen.[75] For the Catholic Guides recruiting suitable leaders would pose a constant problem.

Having weathered the conflict of the early years in establishing a Catholic Guiding organisation over which it could have control, the Catholic church supported a diocesan-based Guiding movement. For the girls, membership of the Guides provided opportunities for travel, education and entertainment that otherwise would not have been open to them. This encouraged a sense of sisterhood amongst the girls and with the provision of a uniform, provided a sense of belonging that disguised class background. The Catholic/Irish ethos of the organisation also ensured that the girls played a part in reinforcing the identity of the state. Through the tenacity of Margaret Loftus and the original committee, who were not afraid to question the church, and through the activities and fun related by the guides who were there, life for some girls and young women in the 1920s and 1930s was stimulating and vibrant.

In the 1940s the Guides became an established feature of Irish society. At that time there emerged an odd disparity in the roles allocated to women. On one level, due to conditions arising because of the war, society accepted that girls and women should participate in duties traditionally carried out by men. However, on another level, during this period the popular view of women as mothers and housekeepers was never more ingrained in the fabric of Irish life.

Notes

1. Patrick Murray, *Oracles of God: The Roman Catholic Church and Irish Politics 1922–37* (Dublin, 2000) p. 10
2. A.J. Gaughan, *Scouting in Ireland* (Dublin, 2006) p. 81
3. P. Stachura, *The German Youth Movement 1900–1945* (London, 1981) p. 19–57
4. Electronic source, Histoclo.com/youth/c1900.htm
5. A.J. Gaughan, *Scouting in Ireland* (Dublin, 2006) pp. 4–5
6. 'Policy and Supporting Material on the Education of Girls and

Young Women in WAGGGS', 1928–1998, CGI Archive, Clanwilliam Terrace, p. 1

7. A.J. Gaughan, *Scouting in Ireland* (Dublin, 2006) p. 81
8. Ibid., p. 83
9. Ibid., pp. 86–8
10. *Memories of Early Days of the Catholic Girl Guides of Ireland* by Sr M. Magdalen, Missionaries of Mary, Betty O'Donovan collection, Clanwilliam Terrace
11. In conversation with Maureen Walsh née Loftus, Greystones, Co. Wicklow, 4 May 2009
12. Dublin Diocesan Archives, Archbishop Byrne Papers, AB8/6/XXI/18
13. Ibid.
14. Henry Boylan, *A Dictionary of Irish Biography* (Dublin, 1999)
15. Dublin Diocesan Archives, papers of Archbishop Edward Byrne AB8/6/XXI/18
16. Diarmaid Ferriter, *The Transformation of Ireland 1900–2000*, p. 335
17. Ronan Fanning, *Independent Ireland* (Dublin, 1983) pp. 39–93
18. Sandra L. McAvoy, 'The Regulation of Sexuality in the Irish Free State 1929–1935', in Greta Jones & Elizabeth Malcolm (eds) *Medicine, Disease and the State in Ireland 1650–1940* (Cork, 1999) pp. 253–65
19. Archdiocesan Archives, papers of Archbishop Edward Byrne, AB8/6/XXI/18
20. Alvin Jackson, *Ireland 1709–1998* (London, 199) pp. 286–7
21. Ibid.
22. Ibid.
23. Ibid.
24. Ibid.
25. *Irish Independent*, Monday, 4 July 1932
26. Ibid.
27. Archdiocesan Archives, Papers of Archbishop Edward Byrne, AB8/6/XXI/18
28. Ibid.

29. Ibid.
30. Ibid.
31. Ibid.
32. Ibid.
33. Ibid.
34. Ibid.
35. Ibid.
36. Letter, 22 November 1934, AB Byrne to Margaret Loftus, courtesy of Maureen Walsh née Loftus, Greystones Co. Wicklow
37. Ibid.
38. Memo of events following on the presentation of the case to His Holiness, Down & Connor Diocesan Archive, Belfast
39. Ibid.
40. Ibid.
41. Legal Documents File, Harrington Street Archive, HSA4
42. UCD Special Collections Dept, James Joyce Library, *Constitution of the Catholic Girl Guides*, 1936
43. Waterford Guide Company History, courtesy of Bríd Rush, Waterford
44. Guide Memories of Camp in Cork, Betty O'Donovan collection, Clanwilliam Archive
45. *Cork Examiner*, The Summer Camp at Clonard Strand, 1934, scrapbook, Betty O'Donovan collection
46. Memories of Camping (Cork), Betty O'Donovan collection, Clanwilliam Terrace
47. *How It All Began*, leaflet, Betty O'Donovan collection, Clanwilliam Terrace
48. Minute book, May McGrath collection
49. A. O'Hagan & Son Solicitors, costs, dated November 1936 to July 1937, legal/Insurance docs, Harrington Street Archive *(HSA from now on)*
50. AB Byrne Hall (CGI Dub. Box) CGI Archive, Clanwilliam Terrace
51. Caitriona Clear, *Women of the House: Women's Household Work in Ireland 1922–1961* (Dublin, 2000) pp. 36–7

52. Diarmaid Ferriter, *The Transformation of Ireland, 1900–2000* (London, 2005) p. 420
53. *The Italian Youth of Catholic Action*, leaflet, undated, HSA3
54. Detlev Peukert, *The Weimar Republic: The Crisis of Classical Modernity* (New York, 1993) pp. 147–81
55. Diarmaid Ferriter, *The Transformation of Ireland, 1900–2000* (London, 2005) p. 420
56. Diary of May McGrath
57. Logbook Buidean Eidín, courtesy of May McGrath
58. Newspaper article dated October 1936, scrapbook, Betty O'Donovan collection, Clanwilliam Terrace
59. Ibid.
60. Betty O'Donovan collection, Clanwilliam Terrace
61. *Irish Press*, 5 April 1934, scrapbook, Betty O'Donovan collection, Clanwilliam Terrace
62. *Irish Press*, 6 April 1934
63. Letters, diary, memorabilia of Betty Casey and others courtesy of Betty O'Donovan
64. *Munster Express*, 13 July 1934
65. Letter from Betty Casey to her aunt, 16 July 1934, Betty O'Donovan collection, Clanwilliam Terrace
66. Kieren Mullarkey, 'Ireland, the Pope and Vocationalism: The impact of the Encyclical *Quadragesimo Anno*' in Joost Augustejn, *Ireland in the 1930s* (Dublin, 1999) pp. 98–116
67. Patrick Murray, *Oracles of God: The Roman Catholic Church and Irish Politics 1922–37* (Dublin, 2000) p. 262
68. Ibid.
69. Diarmaid Ferriter, *The Transformation of Ireland 1900–2000* (London, 2005) p. 408
70. Dáil Debates, Vol. 42, 2 June 1932, Mr Derrig Minister for Education
71. May McGrath Diary, McGrath collection, Catholic Guides of Ireland
72. *Cork Examiner*, June 1932, Betty O'Donovan collection, Clanwilliam Terrace

73. Letter, 30 October 1939, from Michael Clarke, training file 1939–66, HSA
74. Letter, 29 November 1939, Peggy Byrne to Fr Clarke, training file, HSA
75. Report on Religious Examination of Primary Schools in the Diocese of Dublin 1937, HSA4

Chapter 2

Guiding in an Emergency:
Wartime Opportunities and Challenges

1939–1950

*Be prepared and don't be scared
by difficult work or play
to play the fife or save a life
is all in the work of the day.*[1]

The outbreak of war caused considerable uncertainty for people. Although Ireland was neutral, there were fears of invasion from either Britain or Germany. Mr Aiken, Minister for the Co-ordination of Defence Measures, speaking on censorship and the outbreak of war stated:

> Even the abolition of censorship would not prevent the circulation of scare rumours in times like these. The only way to prevent such rumours causing public mischief is to get the people to use their common sense and sense of humour in regard to them and

where a rumour is being spread maliciously or is calculated to damage the safety of the people or of the state, in such a case it is their duty to report the matter to the Gardaí.[2]

Becoming a Guide

By the late 1930s the Catholic Girl Guides had become a feature of Irish society. The organisation was widespread throughout the thirty-two counties and numbers steadily increased. Uniforms, badges and belts were sourced from various suppliers in Ireland and Britain. Quotes for Girl Guide hats were sought from Todd Burns & Co. Ltd, Wholesale and Retail Drapers in Dublin; quotes for badges were requested from A.W. Hewetson Ltd, Embroiderers & Trimming Manufacturers, London; and leather belts were sourced from W.G. Gibson, General Merchant, New Lodge Road, Belfast.

Preparation of a Guide manual was underway after several requests to Ms Sheila Browner, the first Commissioner of the Girl Guides in the Diocese of Dublin, from new companies requesting instruction as to where badges are worn and how they are earned. The aspirant tests formed the basis of the Guide programme and were taken prior to becoming a Guide to ensure a girl was serious about joining a company. A girl could not join the organisation until she was eleven years old and not until she had taken the aspirant tests, which required a Guide to learn and understand the Guide prayer, the Guide principles, the Guide promise and Guide law. There was a special Guide sign and handclasp that could only be given when in uniform. The badge of the Dublin branch of the organisation, designed by Monsignor Myles Ronan, included a combination of the shamrock and the arms of the See of Dublin.

> The Shamrock symbolises the Catholic and Irish heritage of the Guides, and also reminds them of their three-fold Guide Promise. The Archiepiscopal Cross and Pallium remind them of the special loyalty they owe to the Archbishop of Dublin. The Watchword of the Organisation, 'Bí Ullamh', is borne on the horizontal leaves of the Shamrock and a scroll bears the Irish title of the Guides.[3]

After a period of three months and after passing the aspirant tests a girl received her uniform. She then became part of a Guide company and made her promise:

> On my honour with the grace of God, I .... promise to do my best to serve God and Holy Church, to help my neighbour at all times, and to obey the Guide Law.[4]

Once a Guide, further tests followed and, if passed, a badge was awarded that was displayed on a specific part of the uniform. Through Guiding, the Catholic Girl Guides established their own unique identity and as the organisation went from strength to strength they became a visible feature of Irish life. This was evidenced by the grand opening of Archbishop Byrne Hall.

Archbishop Byrne Hall

At the formal opening of Archbishop Byrne Hall at the rear of 36/37 Harrington Street in Dublin, Rev. Monsignor P. Boylan, in his address, cited the founding of the Catholic Girl Guides as 1935, omitting Guiding events prior to this date such as the pilgrimage to Rome in 1934 and the efforts of Margaret Loftus and her associates since 1928. He proudly claimed that the organisation had a membership of 1,500 distributed in companies in 22 parishes of the Diocese of Dublin and he rejoiced in the newly acquired and spacious headquarters in Harrington Street, with the splendid hall equipped with the latest amplification system, including an outdoor speaker installed by the K.D. Radio Electric Company, 'one of the most up-to-date, dignified and impressive Lecture and Concert Halls in Dublin':

> Keen interest in the discipline and reputation of the Companies is kept up by various competitions. The spirit of self-control and cooperation, so greatly needed by our people, is fostered among the Guides by team-games. The importance of Drama as an educational influence is fully recognised by the Guides, and one may hope that the possibilities of

this splendid Hall will be fully exploited in the development of dramatic activity, in both the Irish and English languages, among the Guides.[5]

The opening remarks and a concert performed by the girls were broadcast live on Radio Éireann from the hall, testimony to the status of the Guide organisation in Irish society.

It was proposed to hire out the hall to help it pay for itself. Certain conditions of hire were imposed, for example: a £1 deposit was required, with the balance paid on the night of the performance or function; no card games were to be held in the hall; and the premises had to be cleared by 11 p.m.[6]

Archbishop John Charles McQuaid

As has been seen, the Catholicism of the 1930s was characterised by a church that had contributed to the development of Irish independence and to the building of the new Irish state. This resulted in strong links being forged between churchmen and politicians at an important stage in the state's history.[7] The formulation of the 1937 Constitution is often viewed as a collaboration between church and state. Although Taoiseach, Eamon de Valera sought advice from several clerics, including his friend and neighbour John Charles McQuaid, what he really wanted was church backing without having to grant Catholicism exclusive recognition within the constitution. However, the Catholic church had considerable influence in formulating the articles to do with the role of women, reflecting to a large degree prevailing Catholic concepts of the time.[8] John Charles McQuaid convinced de Valera that women should not have the same kind of rights to work as men, stating 'the law of nature lays diverse functions on men and women'.[9] Therefore Article 41:2 of the 1937 Constitution read:

> The State recognises that by her life within the home, woman gives to the State a support without which the common good cannot be achieved. The State shall, therefore, endeavour to ensure that mothers shall not be obliged to engage in labour to the neglect of their duties within the home.[10]

In 1940 John Charles McQuaid was appointed Archbishop of Dublin by Pope Pius XII. There is evidence to suggest that McQuaid was aware of the difficulties concerning Margaret Loftus and the original organising committee. Judging from the considerable quantity of correspondence, as compared to his predecessor, between him and the Dublin Guide Chaplain, he intended to keep a close eye on all Guide activities.

One of his first acts was to present the Dublin Guides with a gift of £500 to help reduce the debt on Archbishop Byrne Hall. In the third issue of the *Catholic Girl Guide* (1941), the first produced since his appointment to Archbishop, McQuaid published a letter:

Margaret Loftus, President, Catholic Girl Guides of Ireland, in
Guide Uniform c.1932 (photograph courtesy of Mr Seán Loftus)

First enrolment of Catholic Guides at St John
of God's School, Waterford, 1932

Betty Casey diary, 1937

St Colman's Guides from Northern Ireland, 1932

'Just a few of us at the Congress', 1932
(May McGrath collection)

'June', from the logbook of May McGrath, 1932

Guides in early uniform, 1930s

The hike to Ballycorus near Bray, Co. Wicklow, 1932
(May McGrath collection)

Grand Rally, 18 November 1934

Pilgrimage to Rome, 1934 (May McGrath collection)

The Diving Board at Redbarn, 1934

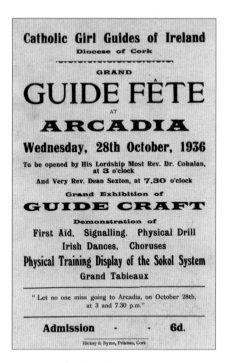

Arcadia leaflet, Cork, 1936

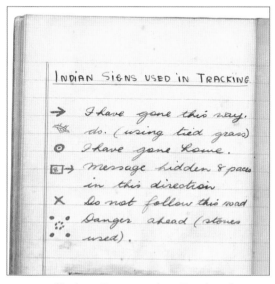

'Indian Signs used in Tracking':
extract from the diary of Betty Casey, Cork, 1937

Building work on Archbishop Byrne Hall, 1939 (photographs courtesy of Harrington Street Archive)

Inside Archbishop Byrne Hall, 1941

Sunday Independent headline reads: '"Peace or War"
Conference: Four Hour Discussion at Herr Hitler's House',
13 August 1939

Potato peelers, Redbarn, Cork, 1940

Maura and Pat Nagel, Cork, 1950

To The CATHOLIC GIRL GUIDES
(DIOCESE OF DUBLIN)
AND THEIR PARENTS

DO YOU KNOW THAT:

1. THRIFT is a trait of Good Citizenship ?
2. It is a means of developing Character, because it demands self-control.
3. A THRIFTY girl makes an economical woman.
4. THRIFT in early years tends to success in later life.
5. Being THRIFTY does not mean being miserly, but enables you to help yourself and others.
6. THRIFT enables a Guide the better to do her duty to God, to her Country and to her neighbour.
7. It helps her to live up to her motto " BI ULLAMH."

The Central Savings Committee consider the present an opportune time to appeal to all citizens to co–operate in a determined "drive" against waste, extravagance and want of thrift.

It cannot be too strongly impressed on the public that it does not follow from the fact that because this country is neutral, we are outside the range of difficulties and hardships arising out of the emergency.

Those things we have to import are ship–borne, and since it is increasingly difficult to secure ships our imports tend to diminish.

Consequently, we must depend more and more on (a) what we can produce at home, (b) what use we can make of "waste" or "scrap," and (c) how economically we can utilise what we have.

Therefore, by example and co–operation we ought to pull together as a family to ensure that carelessness and waste are eliminated from our daily lives.

Foster the "team spirit" in the home and ensure care with a view to securing the most economic use of food, clothing, household goods, light, heat, etc.

By their special training and ideals Girl Guides are specially fitted to help in this important matter.

SEE TO IT NOW.

Leaflets and full particulars of the Savings Scheme on request from the Secretary, Central Savings Committee, Dublin.   No postage needed.

W. H. Co.

Extract from *The Catholic Girl Guide*, 1941

The Guide handclasp

THE FIRST TEST

Know the Elementary Guide Drill

You will find that drill has not a big place in Guiding —the Guide games and outdoor exercises do the work of strengthening your body and of making your carriage all that it should be. Your Company will, however, sometimes appear in public and it is essential that you be able to execute the drill movements properly and smartly.

Fall In :

In single line and "at ease" in the order of your height. Obey quickly and without confusion

Stand at Ease :

Move the left foot six inches from the right foot and to the left, at the same time placing the right hand in the palm of the left hand behind y o u r back — shoulders back, chin up.

Stand Easy :
(Always g i v e n from the "Stand at Ease " position).
Position of feet same as in " Stand at Ease ". Head and h a n d s may be moved. T a l k i n g permitted.

AT EASE

ALERT

Alert :

Bring the left foot smartly into the right and both hands quickly to your sides— thumbs in line with the seams of your skirt. Look straight to the front. Head erect, shoulders back, knees straight. Toes turned out at an angle of 45 degrees.

4

Test: 'Know the Elementary Guide Drill'

Temple Bandage. For wounds on side of head. Place the centre of a narrow-fold bandage on the side *opposite* to the injured one and bind as shown.

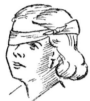

Eye Bandage. Place centre of bandage on bridge of nose and bind as shown. Similar for both eyes, except that end is carried straight back, crossed and knotted in front.

Shoulder Bandage. Place centre of full-sized bandage on shoulder joint with the point well up and lower edge around centre of arm. Pass ends round the arm, cross and knot on the outside. Now secure the forearm in a narrow-fold sling and pass the point of first bandage under and over the sling and pin down as shown.

Hip Bandage. Similar to Shoulder Bandage.

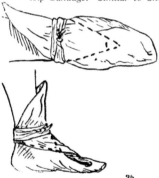

Hand (or Foot) Bandage. Place hand, or foot, on a full-sized bandage and bind as shown, the ends being tied around the wrist or ankle. If the wound is in the palm of the hand, close the hand on the dressing and bandage the closed hand.

25

The Second Class Tests: 'How to bandage a wound'

Dublin bombing, 1941 (photographer unknown)

Advertisement from *The Catholic Girl Guide*, 1941

Map readers, 1940

Trip to Rush, Co. Dublin, 1940

Coming down the mountain, 1941

Corpus Christi procession to Pro-Cathedral, Dublin, 1950
(May McGrath collection)

Dear Father Clarke,

I enclose a contribution towards the Catholic Girl Guides of this diocese and I wish you to use it to reduce your debt in the Bank. This cheque is meant to mark my deep appreciation of the zeal shown by Priests and Lay-workers in an Organisation that particularly appeals to me, because it concerns itself with Primary and Post-Primary Girls. I trust, too, that my small gift is an earnest reflection of the development that I hope for in this work of my saintly predecessor, Archbishop Byrne.

With Kind Regards
John C. McQuaid
Archbishop of Dublin

According to his biographer, Archbishop McQuaid 'urged girls' schools to inculcate in their pupils a Christian reverence for the divine vocation of motherhood to which most of them would be called'.[11] McQuaid insisted that all Guide events be cleared by him in advance. Evidence that he intended to keep a tight control on the Catholic Guides can be seen when he put a stop to a major annual event in the Guide calendar. Every year in May, to celebrate the Feast of Our Lady, all the Guide companies in Dublin came together at Harrington Street and marched in procession to the Pro-Cathedral where they renewed their Guide promise. There was an air of pageantry about the event with a band playing at the head of the procession. In

April 1943, Fr Michael Clarke, Guide Chaplain, wrote to the Archbishop outlining that year's plans for the annual procession. He explained that the entire organisation, including the Reverend Chaplains, were to be in attendance and the Irish Transport and St James' Brass Bands were to accompany the Guide procession, which was to conclude with Solemn Benediction in the Pro-Cathedral. Through his secretary, Archbishop McQuaid forwarded a response the next day, 20 April, which stated:

> The Archbishop does not approve of what is termed the Annual May Procession from Headquarters to the Pro-Cathedral, nor indeed of any parade of adolescent girls in uniform on the public streets or in public play-grounds.[12]

Similarly, through his secretary Michael P. O'Connell, concerning Parents' Day 1945 McQuaid instructed:

> His Grace makes the stipulation that there be no marching or public display parade. If there be dancing he requests that it be in correct costumes and on proper dais and that it not be an exhibitionist programme.[13]

Regardless of these directives, marching and parading continued to be a fundamental feature of all Guide appearances in public.

McQuaid intended to channel Guide activities into the area of social services. Although Ireland was neutral, shortages and rationing were a common feature of the war in southern Ireland. The effects of this for many resulted in poverty, unemployment and emigration.[14] McQuaid had brought together a group of charitable organisations to work together to combat the hardship created by war-time conditions. Social workers from more than forty organisations formed the Catholic Social Service Conference (CSSC). The CSSC was formally inaugurated under McQuaid's patronage. Its four main aims were supplementing and supporting the State during the Emergency; providing a means of employment and supplying the needs of those in distress; channelling public effort and goodwill into a single agency; and mobilising all available resources for the common good.[15]

The CSSC provided food centres in many areas of Dublin. A maternity welfare centre provided medical and nutritional advice including the distribution of baby clothes. Clothing guilds, fuel depots and housing for the poor also came under the umbrella of the CSSC. The Guides participated in these social services by organising cake sales and sales of work to raise money. Material and wool supplied by Fr O'Donnell of City Quay was distributed amongst the Catholic Guide Companies and those with merit badges in sewing and knitting produced garments for distribution to the poor of Dublin. In the report of the Diocesan Chaplain 1944/5 a special tribute was made by Fr Michael Troy to the Guides sewing guild ...

... that has done such excellent work for the poor of City Quay Parish. Our organisation has offered to the CSSC the services of all our Guides who have the Knitter's Badge for the knitting of woollen materials. As soon as supplies are available we shall be given an excellent opportunity of training our members in practical social services.

Impact of War

As far as research can establish, with the outbreak of war Guiding in the North largely seems to have died out, with many Catholic families taking refuge in the south.[16] In some ways Éire became a retreat for northerners seeking a break from the war, and the twenty-six counties experienced something of a holiday boom. Residents of the northern counties were attracted to seaside resorts such as Bundoran in Donegal and Greenore in Louth.[17] South of the border Guide numbers continued to grow, with Guide companies expanding in Cork, Waterford, Tipperary, Kilkenny, Kerry, Limerick, Galway, Tuam and Sligo. In Dublin three companies were enrolled in the Dublin Diocese alone in 1941.

In that year coal supplies from Britain fell sharply and An Taoiseach, Eamon de Valera, instituted a turf-cutting campaign in order to avoid hardship. It was proposed that an extra three million tons of turf be cut that summer. Everyone was called to assist and schools were closed so children could help with the work. May Garvan, a young

Guide in the 1940s, recalled spending a summer during the war cutting turf in the Dublin mountains and singing songs in the back of the truck as it carried the turf to the Phoenix Park.[18] The long straight road through the Phoenix Park in Dublin became known as the 'New Bog Road', as massive mountains of turf were stored there to dry.[19] However, shortages continued and by 1942 long queues for bread were common as imports of flour dwindled. The government launched the 'Grow More Food Campaign' and in 1941 Maura Laverty published a pamphlet titled *Flour Economy*, which gave advice on how to cook scones, bread and pastry economically. Cooking economically was considered a woman's duty, an expression of good citizenship.[20]

Domestic Economy

In June 1941 Archbishop McQuaid and the Minister for Education, Tom Derrig, officially opened St Mary's College, Cathal Brugha Street, where the Archbishop commended the school's teaching of Domestic Economy. He considered it:

> A great thing for the national well-being. He looked forward to the day when schools would advertise the multitude of girls whom they shall have trained, first, to help their mothers at home, and later, to build for themselves a happy home.[21]

McQuaid congratulated the Minister for Education and Dublin Vocational Educational Committee for putting an emphasis on homecrafts as an essential element of women's education. He noted approvingly that the college had been named after 'the Supreme Home-maker and Protectress of Catholic homes'.[22]

Radio Éireann also supported the government's economising campaign and produced a weekly programme for women titled *Scrapbook for Women*, which featured advice on cookery, needlework, gardening, baby care and beauty tips. To instil a sense of patriotism, there were weekly dramatisations of the lives of patriotic Irish women in *Women in History*. A whole series of programmes were produced throughout the war aimed at women, such as *For the Housekeeper* (1941), *Meeting the Wheat Shortages in the Home* (1942) and *Making and Mending in the Home and Habits for Health* (1943). From an educational perspective these programmes had an enormous impact on the lives of ordinary women and led to an increase in membership of organisations such as the Irish Country Women's

Association (ICA), whose activities at that time included craft, cookery and traditional farming. Parish priests regularly enlisted the help of the ICA in running cookery classes in rural areas. The purpose was to teach women and girls how to make meagre ingredients go far.[23]

For the Guides during the war, the merit badge in domestic economy took on a new emphasis and gave instruction in the best ways to cook meat and vegetables, bread and cakes, and even dishes for invalids, including egg flip and steamed custard gruel. Needlework was divided into two aspects: constructive and decorative. House management included instruction on 'efficient methods of doing household tasks'.[24] These tasks would be considered humdrum by today's standards; however, the discipline involved in making ends meet provided an outlet for many women to use their creative skills and develop a sense of purpose at a time when there were few opportunities for ordinary women to exercise their intellectual faculties.

As war restrictions continued, living conditions grew steadily worse in the poorer parts of Dublin. Demands on the CSSC stretched the organisation to the limit. Through the winter of 1942, seven million meals were served through the food centres. To assist, creameries donated milk, butchers gave bones and oxtails, and the farmers of Dublin, Wicklow and Kildare donated sacks of potatoes. Eighty-four clothing guilds produced baby clothes and First Communion and Confirmation outfits. The CSSC distributed five-hundred blankets and warm garments to the elderly and bedclothes to pregnant women. Women in wealthy parishes and former convent schoolgirls, including the Catholic Girl Guides, were encouraged to help clothe the poor.[25]

Thrift

In keeping with the wartime concept of economising, Dr Patrick McKenna, Bishop of Clogher, appealed for participation in the Thrift movement, especially amongst young people. He believed that the elimination of waste and the avoidance of extravagance must be practiced if the country was to survive the strain imposed by war-time conditions. Backed by the Central Savings Committee in promoting the educational and social aims of 'Constructive Thrift' he encouraged the concept be adopted by schools and juvenile groups. The School Savings Association encouraged the saving of small sums by children with a view to the purchase of savings certificates:

> I cannot too strongly emphasise the importance of the 'saving habit' during school years. Adherence to the practice of thrift in early life means that the child leaves school with a sum of money to his credit which he has saved through his own effort which will enable him to make an excellent start in life. Furthermore, membership of a School Savings Association ensures the inculcation of a true idea of the value of money and of the difference between wise and foolish spending – a very useful asset to one about to engage on the important task of earning a living.[26]

Throughout the war advertisements promoting the savings scheme appeared in Catholic Guide newsletters outlining the seven positive traits of thrift.

The advertisement also addressed parents and hoped that they too would play their part and encourage thrifty habits in the everyday life of the home, such as thrift in the matter of health, clothing, household goods and the general avoidance of waste and carelessness.[27] A Guide could earn a merit badge for thrift, but to pass the test she had to demonstrate her ability to save money. She must:

> Have at least 1/- in the Post Office or Savings Bank. You are not to pass this test by getting a shilling from your parents or friends to put into a savings bank. You are expected to save it from money which you usually earn or receive as an allowance. If you can earn the amount so much the better. This shilling should be the start of a steady habit and even if you put only one penny per week into the bank (as the Savings Banks want you to do) you will be learning very well how wise it is to save.[28]

Introducing the Guides to the concept of money management would prove a useful tool for women desirous of financial independence.

Health and Fitness – Military Style

Education for Guides in health and fitness was to the fore in the Catholic Girl Guides, with 'Rules of Health' outlined for members involving fresh air, cleanliness, exercise, food, clothing and rest. Recommended exercise for the girls, along with games, hiking and walking, included complex drilling exercises. Drilling was intended for public appearances only and the drilling exercises were based on the moves of other youth movements from around the world such as the Bengal Guards based in Orange County, Texas.

The Bengal Guards were a school band with 144 girl members including 1 colour guard, 3 drum majors, 7 baton twirlers and 20 flag swingers. Articles on the band outlining their drilling and training techniques were adopted by Guides and became part of their drilling routine. Also of particular interest to the Guides was the 'Sokol Festival Free Exercises for Girls age 9 to 14 years of age'. The Sokols were a militaristic-style gymnastic youth movement from Czechoslovakia who incorporated incredibly complex movements into their drilling.

Reform of the Irish Army had been taking place since the early 1920s. One area of reform concerned physical education. Sokol was the largest gymnastic movement of its time and during the great war the prowess of Czechoslovakian legionnaires was attributed to their membership of Sokol. Following approaches from the

Irish Army the Czechoslovak Ministry of Defence sent Lieutenant Josef Tichy to run courses in Sokol gymnastics and fencing for Irish army officers. Graduates of these courses subsequently taught Sokol in schools and civilian organisations such as the Guides. Sokol's popularity at the time could be compared to the aerobics craze of the 1980s. It was so popular that in 1935 Tichy was asked to speak on Radio Éireann about the origins of Sokol in Czechoslovakia.[29] A considerable number of Sokol exercises were outlined for inclusion in drilling for the Guides.[30] The militaristic aspects are evident in the instructions given, such as 'Fall In', 'Stand at Ease' and 'About Turn'.

According to the handbook:

> When Guides are marching in public they usually march in what is called Company Formation. In order to get Guides into Company formation we do Company drill. By this means, Guides are arranged in threes with the smaller Guides in the centre and the taller ones at the beginning and end of the Company.[31]

The 'March Past' was the most important of the drilling process. This was where the Guides would give a formal salute to an honoured guest.

> On reaching the beginning of the Saluting Base the Captain gives the order Eyes-Right. On this command the entire Company takes one pace, then,

with the exception of the leading Guide of the file nearest the base, all turn their heads smartly over the right shoulder. The leading Guide nearest the base continues to look straight ahead in order to keep the Company marching straight. The Captain as she gives the command, salutes, turning her head to the right. The A/Captain does the same thing – Captains whilst saluting, keep the left arm steady. This position is held until the entire Company has passed the further end of the Saluting Base when the A/Captain then gives the order, Eyes-Front.[32]

The militaristic aspect of the Guides mirrored that of many other youth movements at the time, particularly in Europe. Despite Archbishop McQuaid's dictate concerning Guide appearances in public, there is no evidence to suggest that this prevented the Guides participating in parades other than the May Procession in Dublin. However, as time went on the drilling aspect of the Guide organisation began to fade out.

Accident Insurance

In the annual report produced by the Dublin Diocese in 1939, Fr Michael Clarke had outlined how the war was seriously curtailing Guiding activities. Restricted lighting resulted in classes in domestic economy being cancelled and company meetings were changed to Saturday afternoons to make good use of daylight. However, despite this, many

Guiding activities continued as usual. Occasionally accidents occurred when participating in Guide events. In May 1945 specific insurance had to be sought from the London & Lancashire Insurance Company for the Guides to play camogie:

> the cover would only apply to the risk of injury to Guides whilst playing this game or engaged in any other guide activities to the extent to which the insured have a legal liability for such injury, i.e. there is no question of this cover being on the lines of a personal accident policy.[33]

This was unfortunate for Jenny Ingle who, in May 1946, slipped while playing games at a Guide meeting in Oriel Hall, Seville Place. She sustained a fractured elbow and spent several weeks in Jervis Street Hospital, where she underwent an operation. Jenny was fifteen years of age and worked for Mulcahy Brothers Ltd Hosiery Manufacturers in Clanbrassil Street, Dublin. Her mother complained about the hardship suffered by the family at the loss of Jenny's wages along with hospital and medical expenses. The factory manager, Mr Stokes, agreed to hold her position open for her but the London & Lancashire Insurance Company refused to pay compensation on the grounds that on inspection of the floor at Oriel Hall they could find no reason for her fall.[34]

Because of the regular activity at the Dublin Guide headquarters in Harrington Street, accidents were a constant concern. There was much anxiety regarding instances of fire as many of the rooms were heated by open fires. Fire insurance had been acquired from the Irish Catholic Church Property Insurance Company in 1944 at an annual premium of 31 pounds 10 shillings. This covered 36/37 Harrington Street, which was then valued at £10,000 with contents valued at £1,200. Archbishop Byrne Hall was valued separately at £8,000, with contents including stage, stage scenery and electrical equipment valued at £1,800.

> The above mentioned buildings are lighted by electric light and are heated by a central heating system of hot water pipes and radiators from a coal burning furnace in the basement. It is noted that meetings, evening classes in Domestic Economy, occasional parties, and annual sales of work take place in said buildings. There is a store under the stage in said hall for the storing of the scenery, chairs and other articles. Permission is given for six lantern lectures and six dramatic entertainments to take place annually in the aforesaid hall.[35]

In 1939 Fr Clarke, Dublin Diocesan Guide Chaplain, had proposed to escort over one hundred Girl Guides on a pilgrimage to Lourdes. However, due to the outbreak of war travel was restricted and the trip was postponed. The London and Lancashire Insurance Company cancelled the travel insurance policy.[36] From then on, acquiring insurance for some Guide activities posed a problem. Once war was declared, insurance companies quoted premiums exclusive of war risks. It was stated in the Dáil that insurance companies refused to cover property owners against 'war risk and civil commotion' and that property owners must bear the brunt of the responsibility.[37] As the Guides regularly rented large houses for the summer in which they would camp, the provision of suitable insurance cover became difficult and expensive to acquire. Fundraising ventures such as sales of work and cake sales helped to cover the costs.

Camping the Catholic Guide Way

As mentioned previously the Guides hired a large house in which to camp. Camping was considered an integral part of the Guiding programme during the summer months but was not entirely pursued out of doors or under canvas, as explained in an article titled *In Search of Camp* (1941):

> In the strict sense we do not 'camp'. Cooking and eating all meals in the open, sleeping under canvas, gathering round the great fire in the evening have always appealed to us, but because of the weather and the fact that our 'camp' is available to and used by all the members of the organisation, it has always been thought wiser to use a large residence for our purpose. Nevertheless, it is a rule of camp that we have as many of our activities as possible out of doors. The house is really only a dormitory and refectory.[38]

Every year an annual quest was undertaken by the Guides in Dublin to find a suitable residence for 'camp'. This provided a different setting for the guides to explore each year. Hiking too was a regular and popular feature of Guide life, with trips to Feltrim Hill, Glencullen, Killiney and Kilmashogue. In June 1942 a hike was organised to Bohernabreena.

After taking a bus to Tallaght, then a small village in the countryside surrounding Dublin, the Guides walked to the water-works, where they prepared a meal of sausages and mashed potatoes followed by gooseberries and custard.[39]

While these activities continued to foster a sense of companionship and fun amongst the girls, other activities such as public speaking helped build confidence. In order to obtain a merit badge for public speaking a Guide had to give an original talk of not less than five minutes from notes or complete text to an audience of at least twenty five-people on some phase of Guiding; she had to read a piece of five-hundred words or more that she had never seen before; she had to describe clearly and simply a technical process, i.e. a game or science experiment; and she had to talk impromptu for at least two minutes on a subject of interest to the Guide but chosen by her examiner. Helping girls find their voice was probably one of the most important skills the Catholic Guide organisation passed on to its members.

Guide Leaders

Finding leaders for the organisation was still a problem and Kathleen Gumbrielle, Honorary Secretary of the Dublin Guides, once again appealed to the Catholic Women's Federation of Secondary School Unions for support:

> The fact is that while there are approximately 2,000 girls in this organisation we have not sufficient leaders or senior girls (i.e. over 20 years of age) to undertake these additional, responsible, social activities. We have planned to commence a Course of Training for Cadets who will later qualify for appointment as Captains, and for voluntary workers who will assist in the various Headquarter Committees of the Organisation and with outside public and social work. This Course will begin on Monday, 12 January at 36/37 Harrington Street. It will consist of practical demonstrations and lectures on Guide Work, First Aid, Nature Study, Catholic Action etc.[40]

Advertisements for leaders were placed in the national newspapers and in Catholic Periodicals such as the *Irish Catholic*.[41] The course was intensive: it covered a number of areas and topics and ran over a ten-week period.

> The course will be most comprehensive and will be given by a number of lecturers who are specialists in the various subjects. The subjects of the lectures will

include Catholic Action in its application to Guiding,
First Aid, Company Formation and Practical Guide
Work, Nature Study and out-of-doors, Sokol Drill
etc. There will be no fees or charges of any sort in
connection with the Course. During the Course there
will be a number of Lectures on general subjects and
Travel Talks, illustrated by slides and Guide Films
and visits to Company Meetings and Various Guide
Functions.[42]

Some of the 'specialists' who participated in training
courses for Guides through the forties were Sergeant
Thomas Fegan, School of Physical Culture, Curragh
Camp who gave 'Sokol Instruction' and 'First Aid'
lectures. Louise Gavan Duffy, who was a member of the
original organising committee gave lectures on 'The Art
of Correction' and 'Youth Leadership and its Qualities'.
Maura Laverty gave a series of lectures titled
'Homemaker' and Senator Margaret Pearse (sister of
Patrick Pearse) was asked to give a lecture on 'Our
National Heritage, Language, Song and Games'. Fr F.
Browne SJ, famous for his photographic collection
including photographs taken on the Titanic, gave regular
retreats to the Guides throughout the 1940s.[43]

Wartime Opportunities

Despite the fact that women had, for the most part, been
assigned to the role of homemaker and domestic goddess,

the war years in Ireland provided women with an opportunity to take on roles traditionally dominated by men. Considerable pressure was placed on the Catholic Girl Guides, who were asked to assist with several emergency services such as the Red Cross and St John's Ambulance along with their social work in the CSSC.

On 31 May 1941, German bombers, thinking they were over Belfast, dropped bombs on the North Strand district of Dublin, killing 28 and leaving 2,500 homeless.[44]

In reaction to this the Catholic Guides of Ireland in conjunction with St John's Ambulance service took part in exercises for Guides in fire prevention and fire fighting. Fire rescue included instruction on the fireman's lift and carry, crawling through smoke, how to drag an unconscious person, how to get out of a window and how to go down a partially burnt stairs. In 1944 the Guides also attended a series of lectures given by the Dublin Fire Brigade at Fire Brigade Headquarters in Tara Street, the content of which included first aid, fire prevention, fire fighting and rescue. Merit badges were awarded to Guides for first aid, which incorporated how to treat minor injuries such as sprained ankles, cuts and scratches, fainting and how to effectively dress a wound and apply a bandage.[45]

At this time most of the Guides were of an age where they could work. In a report by the CSSC Youth Council Report (1944) it was found that there was a ...

Gradual increase of female employment in industries where male employment could as satisfactorily, if more expensively, be employed.[46]

The report looked at ways in which women could be kept out of the workforce and replaced by men. It was proposed that a special certificate and badge be awarded to those who passed a three-year course in domestic economy. Concerning typists (a traditionally female-dominated area) the report recommended that a gradual change over to men with a 'minimum fixed wage to be of a man's living standard' be introduced. This shows the widely held assumption that work carried out by women was economically worth less than if men carried out the same work. The report recommended that:

> No girl should be employed before she is eighteen years old in any factory. Up to eighteen years old the training and education should be for the work for which God designed her. Studies in Domestic Economy, Horticulture, Bookkeeping, Dressmaking, Poultry-rearing, Dairying, Home Budgeting, will keep a girl busy in part-time education. Whilst usefully employing a girl up to eighteen years in her proper training for life, this laudable scheme will give more opportunity for those over eighteen for employment.[47]

Not only was it taken for granted that women were paid less for the same job, but the report also proposed to keep girls out of the work force in order to create employment opportunities for unemployed men. Unexpectedly, the Catholic Guides chose to disregard the recommendations of the report and, during the war years, started an employment bureau at Harrington Street to encourage employers looking for staff. Backed by the chaplain, Fr Michael Clarke, captains were requested to provide details on all unemployed Guides who had left school.[48]

There is a certain irony in the fact that the educational programme for the Catholic Girl Guides of Ireland, underpinned by the church, promoted by Catholic social teaching and designed to keep women in the home, should also serve to provide women with the tools required for independent living. It could be viewed that the education the girls received as Guides became somewhat of a double-edged sword. The war years provided the Guides with an opportunity to take on jobs normally carried out by men, such as turf cutting and fire fighting. Money management, public speaking, first aid, health and exercise, and domestic economy provided the knowledge that helped create a body of resourceful and articulate Irish women. These women would pass these skills to their daughters, who consequently may have added to them the ideals of the women's liberation movement of the 1960s and 1970s, a period that would see church control diminishing and significant changes for the role of women in Irish society. For the Guides the 1950s would be a decade where demonstrations of overt Catholicism combined with elaborate theatricals made for some interesting contradictions.

Notes

1. May McGrath Guide logbook, quote 1940, May McGrath collection, CGI Archive, Clanwilliam Terrace
2. Dáil debates, Mr Aiken, Vol. 77, 27 September 1939
3. *The Aspirant Tests* (1945), CGI Archive, Clanwilliam Terrace
4. 1936 Constitution Catholic Girl Guides of Ireland
5. CGI, HSA4
6. Archbishop Byrne Hall, conditions of hire, legal docs, HSA
7. Dermot Keogh, 'Church State and Society', in *de Valera's Constitution and Ours*, Brian Farrell (ed.) (Dublin, 1988) p. 70
8. Dermot Keogh, *Twentieth Century Ireland, Nation and State* (Dublin, 1994) p. 96
9. John Cooney, *John Charles McQuaid* (Dublin, 1999) p. 83
10. *Bunreacht na hÉireann*, 1937
11. John Cooney, *John Charles McQuaid* (Dublin, 1999) p. 111
12. Dublin Diocesan Archives, papers of Archbishop John Charles McQuaid, AB8/6/XXI/18
13. Letter, 26 May 1945, from Michael P. O'Connell, secretary to AB McQuaid to Fr Troy, Guide Chaplain, HSA6
14. Clair Wills, *That Neutral Island: A Cultural History of Ireland During the Second World War* (London, 2007) p. 223
15. John Cooney, *John Charles McQuaid* (Dublin, 1999) p. 115
16. Letters to Dublin from Belfast, CGI, HSA3
17. Clair Wills, *That Neutral Island* (London, 2007) pp. 152–4
18. In conversation with May Garvan; interview held at Our Lady Queen of Peace Nursing Home, Rathgar, 16 September 2008
19. Clair Wills, *That Neutral Island* (London, 2007) p. 238
20. Ibid., p. 242

21. John Cooney, *John Charles McQuaid* (Dublin, 1999) p. 116
22. Ibid.
23. Clair Wills, *That Neutral Island* (London, 2007) p. 243
24. Outline of Instruction on Domestic Economy (1944) CGI, HSA4
25. John Cooney, *John Charles McQuaid* (Dublin, 1999) p. 124
26. Most Rev. Dr McKenna, Bishop of Clogher, *The Thrift Movement*, CGI, HSA4
27. Rally 1939, *To the Catholic Girl Guides of the Diocese of Dublin and their Parents*, CGI Archive, Clanwilliam Terrace
28. *The Second Class Tests* (1945) CGI Archive, Clanwilliam Terrace
29. Daniel Samek, *Czech–Irish Cultural Relations 1900–1950*, Centre for Irish Studies, Charles Univsity (Prague, 2009) p. 47
30. *Sokol Festival Free Exercises For Girls* (from 9–14 years of age), CGI, HSA3
31. *The Second Class Tests* (1945), CGI Archive, Clanwilliam Terrace
32. Ibid.
33. The London & Lancashire Insurance Co. Ltd, 18–19 College Green, legal documents, HSA
34. Letters concerning Jenny Ingle, legal/insurance file, HSA
35. Letter dated 6 July 1944 Arthur O'Hagan & Sons, re fire insurance, Harrington Street, legal/insurance file, HSA
36. Letter to Guides from the London & Lancashire Insurance Co., Ltd, 5 September 1939, legal documents, HSA
37. Dáil Eireann debates, Vol. 77, September 1939, Mr Aiken, Minister for the co-ordination of defensive measures
38. *The Catholic Girl Guide 1941*, newsletter, p.10, CGI Archives, Clanwilliam Terrace
39. May McGrath collection, Guide logbook 1942, CGI Archives, Clanwilliam Terrace
40. Letter, K. Gumbrielle, Hon. Sec., 27 December 1941 training file, HSA
41. Advertisement, *Irish Catholic*, 1940
42. Training course for cadets, training file, 1940/41, HSA

43. Correspondence re. lectures and course plans, training file, HSA
44. Tony Gray, *Ireland this Century* (London, 1994)
45. *Fire Prevention*, CGI, HSA4
46. Catholic Social Services Conference, *Youth Council Report* (June 1944) CGI, HSA4
47. Ibid.
48. Report of Diocesan Chaplain, Fr Michael Clarke, 1944/5, CGI, HSA4

CHAPTER 3

FUN AND FAITH:

ALL KINDS OF CONTRADICTIONS

1950–1960

In the 1950s, the poet Patrick Kavanagh abandoned the crude,
boisterous satire, bred of anger and frustration, which he had
produced in the late 1940s and early 1950s, for a lyrical
celebration of everyday Irish experience that has served for
many Irish men and women since as a metaphor of the surest
kind of liberation, liberation of the spirit.[1]

Ireland in Recession

After the war, Ireland's economy was in crisis. Curbing
emigration was of primary importance to the government and
in 1954 a report commissioned by Mr William Norton,
Tánaiste and Minister for Industry and Commerce, revealed
the causes and extent of emigration that led to a plan for
industrial development. The report found that a principal
reason for emigration was a desire for improved material
standards, together with a dissatisfaction with life on the land.[2]

The Ulster poet John Montague evoked in his poetry what Browne describes as a fairly widespread sense of cultural and social despair.[3] This was reflected in a report by the Department of Finance in 1958 that stated:

> After thirty-five years of native government people are asking whether we can achieve an acceptable degree of economic progress. The common talk among parents in the towns, as well as in rural Ireland, is of their children having to emigrate as soon as their education is completed in order to secure a reasonable standard of living.[4]

The report was written by T.K. Whittaker who was instrumental in regenerating Ireland's weak economy. His economic policies, following on from this report had a profound effect on Irish society over the coming years. Economic growth would develop a sense of urgency in the national psyche that would replace the desire for revival and protection of native language, values and traditions.[5]

Challenges to the Church and Censorship

In the 1950s the church was dealing with the fallout from the Mother and Child scheme, which had the effect of portraying it as uncaring of the needs of mothers and children, and manipulative of government policy. While the 1950s are often identified, from a religious perspective, as having an emphasis on abstinence, fasting and adherence to Catholic festivals, the emergence of a distinct youth culture began to challenge church authority, particularly with the growth in popularity through the 1950s of modern music and dancing. Archbishop McQuaid set up the Vigilance Committee, whose members reported to him evidence of what was considered un-Catholic activity. In 1955 McQuaid was informed of the Mambo Club, where teenagers went to dance to the new rock 'n' roll and where, 'without any supervision anything could happen'.[6] Rock 'n' roll had an immensely liberating impact on men and women in Irish society. For the first time it was no longer necessary to have a partner in order to dance. This relaxed social mores and greatly contributed to the popularity of showbands throughout the country.

The church also encountered considerable criticism concerning its influence in areas such as censorship of film, art and literature by writers and social commentators such as Seán Ó'Faoláin.[7] Censorship was not unique for its time but it was possibly highlighted in a country where educational standards were low and where there was an over-reliance on the church for guidance. It is often thought that censorship was primarily a clerical initiative but the more severe censors were often laymen and the censorship board included Protestant members as well as Catholic. According to Fallon:

> The growing literacy (or semi literacy) of the masses was something relatively new in society, and there was a widespread fear of commercial exploitation of

ordinary people through the medium of print – and, of course, through the cinema.[8]

Plays, however, were relatively uncensored. Playwright Paul Vincent Carroll, born in County Louth, had won considerable acclaim for his plays *Shadow and Substance* and *White Steed*, winning the New York Drama Critics Award for best foreign play in 1937 and 1938. According to his biographer he was 'the most important dramatic talent in the Irish theatre since the early writings of O'Casey'.[9] Carroll spoke openly about his dissatisfaction with cultural life in Ireland, claiming:

> They fed the school kiddies on the bathos of the mid-Victorian mamas and hid from them the works of the poets and writers who were putting Ireland on the international map.[10]

Carroll held the perception that cultural life in Ireland was stagnant and stifled by strict clerical control. But not all children were sheltered from modern Irish culture. Two of Carroll's plays for children were amongst the records of the Catholic Girl Guides of Ireland.[11] There is a sense that the Catholic Girl Guide organisation, whilst appearing to conform to general social trends, often quietly ignored them. Like the employment bureau in the 1940s, when it would have been in keeping with the organisation's status, under the umbrella of Catholic Action, to support the findings of the report, they chose to ignore it. It is unlikely that this was recognised as a rebellious trait. The technique was probably adopted by many women at a time when they were not encouraged to dissent. It was perhaps considered a normal means to an end.

Also in keeping with its status under Catholic Action would have been support of censorship of anything deemed indecent. However, this appears not to have been the case: although the Catholic Guides were lobbied for support, as far as research can establish these approaches were disregarded. The Catholic Guides were propositioned by various organisations to support calls for censorship in one form or another. At the time there was considerable concern by lay Catholic organisations regarding standards of decency. In 1952, the Catholic Women's Federation of Secondary School Unions wrote to the Guides seeking their support for a letter they intended to distribute to public authorities in charge of coastal districts and to the daily papers. The Federation was concerned that the development of the tourist trade was having a negative influence on the people of Ireland:

> The development of the tourist trade is bringing visitors of many nationalities to Ireland, and as one of the most Catholic Countries in the world it should be our pride to set a standard for seaside behaviour.[12]

The Federation wanted the local authorities to formulate rules for the use of beaches that included facilities for separate dressing for men and women and standard regulation swimming costumes for swimming and sun-bathing.[13]

Similarly, the Irish League of Decency also sought the support of all Catholic organisations including the Guides to back them in their efforts to 'combat indecency' when they called for a 'tightening up of censorship of books and periodicals'.[14] There is no evidence to suggest why the guides did not respond to these calls for support. There is no doubt the Catholic guide organisation was conservative. It may have been that asking young girls to support anything pertaining to indecent behaviour was indecent in itself and therefore they were not inclined to get involved.

International Facets of Catholic Guiding

Although quietly extricating itself from involvement in calls for censorship, the Guiding programme still reflected the Catholic ethos that permeated Irish society at the time. Participation in religious events such as Corpus Christi processions, devotions in honour of St Brigid and pilgrimages to Knock shrine were part of everyday life in Ireland in the 1950s. It was reported in the *Irish Independent* that a pilgrimage of about 20,000 of the youth of Ireland gathered at

Knock for the annual children's pilgrimage. The report claimed they represented practically every school, convent, college and university in the country.

> The 4th Mayo Troop, Boy Scouts under Scout Leader J. Morley and the 2nd Galway Troop from Tuam under N. Loftus as well as units of the Catholic Girl Guides acted as guard of honour when the diamond studded statue of Our Lady was carried at the head of the procession.[15]

As in previous decades, visits to places of pilgrimage such as Rome and Lourdes provided the girls with opportunities for travel.

At Easter 1950, chaplain Fr Thackaberry led a Guide pilgrimage to Rome with forty-nine officers and Guides. The trip included visits to London, Paris and Turin with stop-offs along the Italian Riviera. The highlight, however, was an audience with Pope Pius XII in St Peter's Square where 40,000 devotees were in attendance shouting '*Viva Il Papa*'.[16] In her Guide logbook, May McGrath recorded a visit to her company from Fr Thackaberry, who had just returned from the trip:

> ... he had lots to tell us. The Guides were very interested and kept creeping up nearer to him every few minutes. They asked questions for ages and admired his gold Guide badge. When he looked at his watch it was 9.30 p.m. so he ran away and told them to write their questions out for next week.[17]

While the devotional aspects of the trip would have been of interest to the girls there is no doubt that foreign travel, which had been restricted during war time and considered something only well-off people could do, would have been seen as very exotic. A letter from Aer Lingus, the Irish airline, to the Guides claimed that the

> Introduction of Viscounts on the Lourdes service will, of course, enable us to carry many more passengers – perhaps your entire pilgrimage – in greater comfort and in a flying time of approximately three hours.[18]

In 1958 the *Evening Press* reported on the pilgrimage to Lourdes:

> A party of 200 Catholic Girl Guides will leave Dublin by special planes for Lourdes on Easter Sunday. They will spend four nights in Lourdes before proceeding to San Sebastian for a visit to the Shrine of St Ignatius at Loyola.[19]

Other opportunities for travel occasionally presented themselves when organisations such as the International Auxiliaries sent representatives to Ireland in the 1950s to seek lay workers in the Belgian Congo and the Irish Secretariat of the European Youth Campaign distributed information on conferences held in Paris and the Netherlands.

Encouraged by Archbishop McQuaid, the Catholic Guides made efforts to liaise with other Catholic groups around the world to promote and further Catholicism. Pax Christi was a movement founded in 1945 by Cardinal Feltin, Archbishop of Paris. Its aim was to promote goodwill between the nations 'and in particular mutual understanding and esteem friendship and brotherhood between the Catholics of the world'.[20] The organisation served as a centre for the exchange of correspondence, a kind of 'pen-pal' service where Catholics could communicate with other Catholics from around the world.

The international theme of the 1950s continued when, in April 1953, the World Federation of Catholic Young Women and Girls held a week-long international conference in Ghent, the subject of which was 'Catholic International Doctrine on International Relations and European Questions'.[21] Captain Yvonne Robins was the Catholic Guide delegate chosen to attend.[22] This organisation encouraged women to pay attention to international matters and promote understanding through 'friendship camps' and the study of languages. In 1958 the newsletter of this body quoted the Rev. Peter Kitter on the subject of the mission of the modern Christian woman:

> She must be a dispenser, protectress and succourer of life – giving in her own heart, shelter to little ones, support to the weak, a refuge to those in danger, rescue to the stranded. (Rev. Peter Kitter, D.D., *Christ and Womankind*, Newman Press, Westminster 1952)[23]

The newsletter went on to explain:

> This is why woman perverts herself when she strives simply to imitate man or assumes a false equality which takes no account of the fundamental differences in their missions.[24]

This shows that, as in previous decades, the Catholicism that assigned women to the role of homemaker and mother was not unique to Ireland. This World Federation, based in Belgium, mirrored views held by many clerics and lay Catholics throughout Europe.

Trendsetting Youth Movement of the 1950s

In contrast to the intense religiosity of the times reflected in the Catholic Guide organisation, a series of Gilbert and Sullivan Operas was performed by the Guides throughout the 1950s. The rights to the operas were held by the D'Oyly Carte Opera company based in London and permission to reproduce was sought well in advance of each performance. The opera company was entitled to a percentage of the receipts taken at the door, so considerable effort went into selling tickets and filling the hall. The performances were elaborate affairs, with theatrical costumes sourced from as far away as London. *HMS Pinafore* was produced by Michael McGreal, with musical director Moira Griffith. It was performed in 1950 with costumes provided by Gings Theatrical Stores on Dame Street. Over the course of the decade, performances of *The Gondoliers*, *Iolanthe*, *The Mikado* and *The Pirates of Penzance* were staged at Archbishop Byrne Hall and received much media coverage. The *Dublin Evening Mail* on Saturday, 27 November 1954 reported:

> The Catholic Girl Guides of the Archdiocese of Dublin presented the 'Pirates of Penzance' with an all female cast at the Archbishop Byrne Hall. The best feature was the chorus, which always looked as if it knew why it was on the stage. Michael McGreal secured a commendable production and the orchestra conducted by Moira Griffith despite a few anxious moments acquitted itself creditably.[25]

Careful attention to singing was evident in the report made by the critic who proffered this opinion regarding the performance of *The Gondoliers* in 1957 in the *Dublin Evening Mail*:

> Some really fine singing from principals and chorus was heard in this thoroughly enjoyable production. All voices, without exception, were of good quality. The chorus not only sang well, with excellent articulation and good tonal blend, but displayed an unusual and welcome sense of humour when required.[26]

Throughout the 1950s the Guides regularly featured in the national daily newspapers, where their attendance at flag blessings, pilgrimages, commissioning of Guide officers and parents' days were popular features. They often participated in radio programmes on the national radio station. In 1955 they took part in a quiz show called *Watch the Clock,* broadcast on Friday, 4 March on Radio Éireann. In this episode Catholic Girl Guides competed with Catholic Boy Scouts during a recording of the launch of the quiz. Catholic Guides and Scouts were also invited to ask questions of a panel of experts during the programme *It's All Yours*, which was broadcast on Friday, 1 April 1955.[27]

Parents' Days

The annual parents' days provided an opportunity for the Guides to showcase what they had learned through Guiding. The event was widely publicised in the national newspapers and many high-profile guests were invited to attend as guest of honour. In Dublin, permission was sought from Prof. Michael Tierney, President of UCD, to hold the event in Iveagh Gardens, part of the Earlsfort Terrace premises at the National University (UCD). In 1949 the Guides requested an army bugler from the Department of Defence to announce the opening of the event. Performances were given by pipers from the Catholic Boy Scouts and, while the line-up varied over the years, it generally included raising of flag, parade and inspection, games, competition, Guide drill display and a presentation of shield and cups.[28]

By this time Guides were at the height of their popularity, with a large and growing membership. It has been difficult to establish how many members exactly there were at its peak in the 1950s but it is estimated that at one time during this period there were 10,000 members in Dublin alone. They had become an important part of Irish society. This is evidenced by the considerable publicity they received through the media and by the important guests who attended the Parents' Day events. On the 6 July 1953, under the headline 'Gaelic Culture Guides' Goal', the *Irish Press* reported:

> The efforts of the Catholic Girl Guides, Dublin Diocese, for the language were explained to the parents and friends of the Guides at the annual Parents' Day celebrations in Iveagh Gardens yesterday by the Diocesan Chaplain, Very Rev. C. Troy, P.P. ... The organisation endeavoured by its training to instill a true Christian culture in the Guides, a culture that was not merely Christian but Gaelic. Fr Troy said, stress was placed on the Irish language and some of the Guide companies were all Irish speaking.[29]

The high-profile guests who attended the Parents' Day events and gave stature to the organisation included the Argentine Ambassador to Ireland, Señor Lorenze McGovern and his wife, who in 1956 'took the salute of over 2,000 Guides who later presented folk dancing, figure marching and drill and two pageants'.[30] In 1957 the Honorary Guest at the Iveagh Gardens display was Mdme

De Blesson, wife of the French Ambassador, who presented prizes to the Guides.[31] In 1958 the Countess De Laubespin, wife of the Belgian Ambassador, 'inspected 60 companies of the Catholic Guides who gave exhibitions of musical drill, folk dancing, precision marching and performed a pageant of Our Lady of Lourdes before four hundred parents and guests'.[32] The pageants provided an opportunity to demonstrate and emphasise a distinct Irish culture and identity in front of foreign political figures. The Catholic Guides had become so widely respected they were entrusted with reinforcing Ireland's cultural identity, as well as being given responsibility for forming young minds that reflected a uniquely Irish way of life.

Fernhill

While the Guides entertained the country with public displays, theatrics and radio broadcasts, simultaneously the traditional Guide activities were being pursued.

Camping was the highlight of the summer for the Catholic Guides. In 1950 and 1951 Ballynerrin House and Glen Cottage in Wicklow were considered suitable for camps. However, encouraged by Archbishop McQuaid the Guides decided to purchase a permanent residence for camping purposes. McQuaid donated £500 towards this venture. In June 1953, Fernhill, Co. Wicklow, was purchased and was ready for camp in August of that year. It was situated close to the sea, hills and Wicklow town, and was surrounded by seven acres of land. The Catholic Guide organisation was open to girls from all walks of life, as can be seen from a letter written in 1958 by Guides to the commissioners and captains of the organisation complaining about the costs of camping and hiking. For most of the girls the camp was the only holiday they got as children. This letter (reproduced in full) demonstrates the diverse backgrounds from which the girls came and the times in which they lived.

3rd July 1958

Dear Commissioners & Captains,

1. *We hope you will not think us forward in writing this letter, but we thought you might like to know what a lot of the Guides are talking about. There are two things in particular that we would like you to consider:-*

2. *This thing about Guides paying full fare down to Camp, and on Hikes. What about the Guides who are still going to school, it takes them all their time to get the money for Camp, without having to pay full fare on the bus. After all most Guides at school of sixteen years of age, can easily pass for half fare. We all know why this rule was made, but why not think of the Parents who have to pay for the fares. Some Guides have two and three sisters in the organisation, well their parents could not be expected to give them full fare. It is ridiculous going on a hike, a Guide still at school having to pay full fare.*

3. *We believe that the organisation was presented with another cup. Well we would like to give a suggestion. Could this cup not be for 'Arts and Crafts'. This would enable the ordinary working Guide to have a chance of winning something. A girl leaving school at 14 and going to work at sewing or in a factory, has not a chance of going in for many cups. If this cup could be presented for 'Arts & Crafts', well these Guides would enter a frock (hand made) a tablecloth (embroidered) or anything like that. Most Guides who went to Lourdes were only ordinary working Girls.*

Hoping you will consider this matter, and give it your most considerate attention.

HOPEFUL[33]

This letter shows the solidarity that existed amongst the girls and the mix of working and schoolgoing Guides within the organisation.

The Guides' involvement in events at a community level such as religious ceremonies, festivals and parents' days made them a very visible feature of Irish society. Being a Guide was considered a worthy role for a respectable Catholic girl. The Guides avoided controversy by being neutral on issues such as censorship but were certainly Catholic enough for it to be assumed that they followed general trends in that regard. With few alternatives, Catholic Guiding in the 1950s provided many opportunities for girls and young women. In contrast to the popular portrayal of life for Irish women in the 1950s as being suppressive, the Catholic Guide organisation provided opportunities for travel, drama and social activity.

In the early 1960s two events would have a major impact on Irish society and signal a departure from the past. Vatican II peeled away the mystery shrouding the Catholic church, leaving it open to question whilst, simultaneously, the widespread popularity of television provided a forum for questioning. Irish society, including the Catholic Girl Guides would have to adapt to a new modernity.

Notes

1. Terence Browne, *Ireland: A Social and Cultural History, 1922–2002* (London, 2004) p. 216
2. Government commissioned report (William Norton), Causes and Consequences of the Present Level and Trend in Population, 5 April 1954, Official Documents Dept, UCD
3. Terence Browne, *Ireland: A Social and Cultural History, 1922–2002* (London, 2004) p. 201
4. Ibid.
5. Ibid., p. 202
6. John Cooney, *John Charles McQuaid* (Dublin, 1999) p. 232
7. Peter Lennon, *Rocky Road to Dublin*, 1968 (documentary)
8. Brian Fallon, *An Age of Innocence: Irish Culture 1930–1960* (Dublin, 1998) p. 206

9. Paul A. Doyle, *Paul Vincent Carroll* (New York, 1971) p. 17
10. Ibid.
11. Ibid.
12. Letter to Guides, 16 June 1952 from Maeve Donovan, Hon. Sec. Catholic Women's Federation, HSA
13. Ibid.
14. Irish League of Decency (2 letters) 13 July 1958 and 16 November 1958 re. censorship to Guides, HSA
15. *Irish Independent,* May 1955
16. *Ecco Roma,* An banóglac 1955, CGI, HSA3
17. May McGrath collection, Guide logbook, CGI Archive, Clanwilliam Terrace
18. Aer Lingus letter to secretary CGI, 4 October 1956, from J.R. Leonard, sales manager, HSA5
19. *Evening Press,* 29 March 1958
20. Pax Christi, CGI, HSA3
21. Women and Europe, CGI, HSA3
22. An banóglac 1955, CGI, HSA3
23. *World Federation of Catholic Young Women and Girls,* Newsletter (HSA3)
24. Ibid.
25. *Dublin Evening Mail,* Saturday, 27 November 1954
26. *Dublin Evening Mail,* Monday, 4 March 1957
27. *Irish Independent,* radio review, Friday, 1 April 1955
28. Parents' Day Programme, Parents File, HSA
29. *The Irish Press,* 6 July 1953, Parents' Day, HSA4
30. *The Irish Press,* 6 July 1956, Parents' Day, HSA4
31. *The Irish Press,* 15 July 1957 Parents' Day, HSA4
32. *The Irish Press,* 7 July 1958, Parents' Day, HSA4
33. Letter from Guides to Commissioners and Captains, 3 July 1958, HSA3

CHAPTER 4

THE NEW MODERNITY:

ADAPTING TO CHANGE

1960–1979

*In a society where the rights
and potential of women are
constrained, no man can be
truly free. He may have power,
but he will not have freedom.[1]*

Changes in the Church

In the 1960s the second Vatican council underlined change for the Catholic church with alterations to the form of the mass sparking controversy between clergy and lay people alike. Former Chief Commissioner Betty O'Donovan recalled meetings being held in her local parish concerning Vatican II:

> This was a time of very big change ... I remember it was something that I was very taken with, I thought it was great, but there was a lot of people who missed the Latin and didn't like the idea of it going

and even still the older people would miss it. But I thought it was great and it seemed to open up the Church and make it more modern.[2]

It was becoming obvious that the role of the priest was changing too and a new approach to Catholicism by younger priests was beginning to emerge. Fr Michael Cleary (often referred to as the singing priest) was a controversial figure. He was regularly used by the church as a spokesman on controversial matters such as contraception and celibacy.

With the economic boom and the introduction of the hire-purchase scheme, televisions were flooding into homes around the country, fast becoming the most popular form of entertainment. Cleary was a regular guest on the popular weekly *Late Late Show*, which provided a forum for those with views on Irish society.[3] Judging from public reaction to programmes such as these, it was becoming clear that church power was diminishing, being questioned and adapting to a new social order. This created conflict within the church on how to cope with the changes of the 1960s.

According to Fr Brian D'Arcy there was concern for the moral well-being of youth, which provided the reasoning behind the extreme reactions of some clergy to the new modernity:

> There is always fear of modernity, but it is not only within the church. Every human being who lives to the age of maturity fears change. And when change involves a complete restructuring of society and morality, then it's no wonder people feared its influence. In society and

in the Church there was an unhealthy fear of the new which became an obsession. It was more about power than about mature moral choices.[4]

Changes in Guiding

Some of the Guides who joined in the 1960s and rose through the ranks of the organisation noted the changes that started to emerge. Guiding had come to the Diocese of Ferns in 1945 with St Aidan's the first company of Guides formed in Wexford town. Mary Lawlor joined in 1965 at the age of eleven:

> Myself and a couple of friends, Martha and Marion arrived at the Guide Hall, in those days the meetings were from 7.30 p.m. to 9 p.m. My original motive wasn't completely genuine as I joined more or less to please my Dad but here I am 30 years later and still as enthusiastic as ever.[5]

Mary has fond memories of being a Guide and is extremely grateful now to her Dad for making her go. Caroline McGuinness joined the Guides in 1968 and she too has many happy memories of Guiding in Wexford:

> My earliest memory of Guiding were the hikes out to Ardcavan Beach, we would leave the Corish Memorial Hall at about 10 a.m. and hike all the way to Ardcavan along the beach, when we got there we would make a campfire and cook sausages and beans. We would also

have a swim and before we left for home we would have a sing-song at the campfire, these were great days.[6]

Caroline's memories of Guiding were happy and as she progressed through the organisation into positions of responsibility she wanted to share her experience with the girls in her charge – 'but it wasn't easy, times were changing and the strict disciplinary ways of Guiding were drifting away'.[7] Guide leaders were finding it increasingly difficult to incorporate a sense of discipline into Guide activities, possibly because they were now being challenged by a more questioning and better-educated generation of girls.

In 1966 the Minister for Education, Donogh O'Malley, introduced free secondary education. O'Malley was acting on figures revealed in a United Nations Educational, Scientific and Cultural Organisation (UNESCO) report that showed only 36 per cent of Irish children aged 14 to19 attended secondary or technical schools, half the rate of some other European countries and well behind that of Northern Ireland.[8] O'Malley stated:

> Every year, some 17,000 of our children finishing their primary schools course do not receive any further education. This means that almost one in three of our future citizens are cut off at this stage from the opportunities of learning a skill and denied the benefits of cultural development that go with further education. This is a dark stain on the national conscience, for it means that some one third of our

people have been condemned – the great majority through no fault of their own – to be part educated unskilled labour, always the weaker who go to the wall of unemployment or emigration.[9]

Changes in the Role of Women

In the 1960s the Irish Country Women's Association and the Irish Housewives Association, two organisations often considered to have a conservative image, joined other women's groups to form a committee on women's rights. Their extensive lobbying led to the establishment of the first Commission on the Status of Women in 1970.[10] Increasingly, women called for greater equality, particularly in the workforce where in 1961 women accounted for only 29 per cent.[11] The outspoken feminist, June Levine, articulated the frustration felt by women:

> the sixties were a good time for the boys. Lemass's Ireland was flourishing, business booming, high hopes. There was money around, and employment and optimism. And if one had been a mite more sensitive, it would have been possible to recognise the anger that was mounting under the surface as the decade went on. It was female anger, subtle, veiled but there ... It was an anger which clearly said: 'ok the awful fifties are gone, things were going right for a change. Going right for the boys. But what about us?'[12]

One member of the Catholic Guides recalled that in the 1960s when a Guide got married she was expected to resign from the organisation. In 1965, she received a letter, including a picture of the Sacred Heart, from the Dublin Diocesan Secretary stating that her services were no longer required.[13] This mirrored the state ban on married women working in the Public Service that was not removed until 1973, coinciding with Ireland's membership of the EEC. However, probably the most visual evidence of change from the 1950s to the 1960s came in the form of women's fashions. For women, the fashion style of the 1960s symbolised liberal attitudes and was associated with female emancipation. However, for many women, perceptions of liberation were often a double-edged sword, as articulated by Coote and Campbell:

> It is true that the sixties' counter-culture challenged a lot of old ideas and allowed new ones to blossom; thus far, it nourished the roots of emergent feminism. But at the same time it added a new dimension to the oppression of women, setting them up, in their mini-skirts and mascara, in a gallery of new toys with which men were now free to play.[14]

The shorter skirts of the Guide uniform and the trendy sunglasses worn by some of the girls (see colour section) were in keeping with the fashions of the time.

Changes in Youth Culture

In the 1960s it became generally acknowledged by the church and society that teenagers now represented a distinct group. This demonstrated a significant change from the 1950s to the 1960s. Teenagers became big business. A study undertaken in Britain and published in 1960 estimated that for every five young people between the ages of 15 and 20, there would be six young people by 1964.[15] Many articles expressed concern about Irish teenagers such as the one from *Christus Rex*. The author, Walter Forde, believed that Irish teenagers were being negatively influenced by English trends.

> Their general characteristics and life are well known, their addiction to jazz and pop music. Their world centres on coffee-bars and juke boxes, on motor bikes and gang life, on cafes and cinemas. Mass teenage demonstrations are frequent news headlines. In general they are very cynical towards service, either of the community or of individuals. Their fashions in clothes and hair-styles increasingly follow English trends. The amount of money spent by them on records, dances and clothes is a new feature of Irish life. Drinking among them too is becoming common.[16]

Barbara Goodall Wallace, a Guide in Wexford in the 1960s would probably disagree with Forde's assessment.

> 'Left, left, left right left', the voice comes authoritatively from behind. 'Swing your arms, hold up your heads,

keep in line'. For what seems like the hundredth time we march up and down, fall in, fall out, number by threes, form threes, right turn, about turn by the left – and off we go again. Corpus Christi Procession time, An Tostal or St Patrick's Day is near and we have to practice for what seems like hours every evening beforehand. No it's not the Irish Army. It is a group of young girls from 11 years of age up to the early twenties. St Aidan's 1st Wexford Troop of Catholic Girl Guides to be precise.[17]

However, in Ireland due to the economic upturn and the drop in emigration, teenage spending power was growing, highlighting a rich market for exploitation by manufacturers and advertisers. This was testimony to the economic policies of the Lemass-led government, which were a great success and were complimented by President John F. Kennedy when he addressed the Oireachtas during his state visit on 28 June 1963:

> You have modernised your economy, harnessed your rivers, diversified your industry, liberalised your trade, electrified your farms, accelerated your rate of growth and improved the living standard of your people. Other nations in the world in whom Ireland has long invested her people and her children are now investing their capital as well as their vacations here in Ireland. This revolution is not yet over, nor will it be, I am sure, until a fully modern Irish economy fully shares in world prosperity.[18]

Adapting to Change

By the mid-1960s the economic boom had encouraged the development and expansion of towns and cities, with suburban housing estates being built at a great rate. Travel became easier and more affordable, with Aer Lingus laying on direct flights to places of pilgrimage.

In May 1960 the *Cork Examiner* gave an insight into some of the highlights of the trip for the girls during a pilgrimage to Rome. The evening before they were due to return home they were given a walking tour of the eternal city:

> Many of them will remember the palace of Caesar lit by soft amber lights, the gloom of the Broken Bridge where once brave Horatio stood in defence of Rome; the menacing heights of the Tarpean Rock with its unpleasant memories; the brightness of the Capitol Hill and the Senate House where history was planned ... the Trevi Fountain whose cascading waters devoured the Irish girls' coins. These are memories to be cherished.[19]

The experience of foreign travel was still very new and provided a marvellous opportunity for all Guides regardless of their ability to pay. Fundraising events covered the fares of about half the group with names being pulled from a hat for the allocation of places on the trip. The Catholic Guides reflected and adapted to changes during a decade of considerable social upheaval. The historian, David Thornley, writing in 1964, found it incredible that such a large proportion of Irish society was prepared so easily to abandon the policies of the past and accept economic growth and modernity. He believed these changes to have been brought about as a result of a 'delayed peaceful social revolution'.[20]

In the 1960s, within the Guide Association, there is evidence of increased communication between the different diocesan-based Catholic Guide organisations from around the country working together to share ideas concerning Guiding. Evidence of this was seen at a Guiding Seminar organised on 3 April 1966 at the Grand Hotel in Malahide. Representatives from Belfast, Larne, Limerick, Cork, Carrick-on-Shannon, Athlone and Arklow attended, and a variety of workshops were organised on topics such as Out-of-Doors and Knots & Games. Significantly, Beatrice Dixon, Area Commissioner of the Irish Girl Guides (the other Guiding organisation operating in the Republic), was asked to give a talk on an aspect of Guiding and she accepted. This shows that communication links were being fostered not only between the dioceses within the Catholic Guide organisation itself, but with other Guiding organisations.

As the Catholic Guides sought to engage with similar organisations so too did Ireland but on a much bigger scale. On 1 January 1973, Ireland joined the European Economic Community (EEC). Support for membership was strong, with Ireland set to gain economically from association.[21] At the Guides' annual Parents' Day, held once again in the Iveagh Grounds in 1973, the programme included dances representative of EEC countries, together with a variety of exhibitions on EEC countries that were displayed by the Guide companies. An *Evening Herald* reporter stated:

> Until yesterday I had only a dim idea of the many accomplishments of a senior Guide. She's good at games, first aid, cookery and other domestic crafts, nature study and signalling. She's also strong on history, liturgy, verse speaking and public speaking, not to mention floral arrangement and the ability to organise a rousing sing-song round a camp-fire. To all that add sewing, embroidery and a flair for producing plays and acting in them and you have a girl any chap would be a damn fool not to marry. At the annual Parents' Day for the Guides ... the theme of the day was the EEC. The Brigins danced the native dances of the Common Market countries and the Guides exhibited the arts and crafts of the aforementioned group of nations.[22]

New Dangers

The Catholic Girl Guides were embracing foreign cultures and displaying an openness to foreign influences, a marked departure from the demonstrations of an Irish cultural revival of the recent past. In an address to commissioning officers of the Catholic Girl Guides given by the newly appointed Archbishop Dermot Ryan on 20 May 1973, the Bishop outlined the concerns of a modern Irish society now noticeably different from the past:

> Being a member of the Guides helps you to be generous, to think of other people, to be unselfish. That is what brings happiness. Selfish pursuit of what you want or expecting that you can get everything you want produces unhappiness. Self control is necessary in our attitude to alcohol, drugs and to sex. Lack of self control in the sexual order ultimately shows a lack of reverence for the mystery of motherhood and new life.[23]

The Church was no longer concerned with 'Thrift' and 'Domestic Economy' but with the dangers to girls brought about by the excessive use of alcohol, drugs and sex, side-effects of a modern, affluent society. This was reflected too in changes made to the Guide programme within the organisation, which responded to the demands from girls for a more challenging line-up of courses including the introduction of merit badges for geologist, fire fighter, chemist and sportswoman.[24]

Secularisation of schools was debated in the media. An article in the *Irish Independent* highlighted this when it reported that, at a meeting of the Congress of Catholic Schools, Mr Patrick McCarthy strongly defended the value of denominational schools. He stated that his organisation:

> did not oppose the right of any viable group of parents to opt for any particular type of school, but they did oppose the attempts of a hostile, well-publicised minority, to impose upon the majority a monolithic secularised state controlled system of education.[25]

North and South

North and south of the country, Seán Lemass and Terence O'Neill both fostered belief in a new era, and raised expectations amongst disenfranchised groups that prosperity would be accompanied by liberalism and tolerance.[26] Looking back, this was considerably wide of the mark. In Northern Ireland during the war, Catholic Guiding had almost died out, but in the mid-1960s it experienced unprecedented growth. Catholic suppression meant communities were divided by religion and literally by barricades. Because of the political situation at the time it would have been impossible for Catholic girls to join the BP (Baden Powell) Ulster Girl Guide Association, who were perceived as a Protestant-only organisation. The problems for Catholics were outlined by Fr Padraig Murphy to Bishop Philbin in a memorandum titled, *Points of the discussion on the proposal that Catholic girls in Northern Ireland should join the BP (Baden Powell) Girl Guides Association.* The document stated that up until 1966 'with few exceptions, the BP Guide Association in Northern Ireland was made up of members from the Protestant community'.[27] He stated that there was a lot of interest in Guiding in Catholic schools but that there were three main issues he identified that posed problems for Catholics: the promise, the flag and the uniform. The promise a girl had to make on joining included an oath of loyalty to the Queen but, as the author explains,

> The fact is that the name and image of the Sovereign has a quite different significance here as compared with any other part of the commonwealth. Elsewhere it is the symbol of unity; here it is employed as a weapon of division.[28]

The memo described how the Queen was 'invoked and honoured at anti-Catholic rallies' and that this was tolerated and supported by the establishment. It was felt that there was little possibility of the BP Ulster Guiding Association adapting their promise, as it would be seen as an act of disloyalty while at the same time, in its present form, was unacceptable to Catholics.

The memo also outlined how the flag (Union Jack) too was viewed by Catholics as a symbol of division. 'It is seen as the flag of a party, the Unionist Party, which in turn is dominated by the Orange Order, well known for its anti-Catholic sentiments.' Cited were examples of many instances where the Union Jack flag was used as a symbol of divisiveness and as such, according to the memo, it was understandable that Catholics would not want to belong to an organisation with an emblem that rejected them and their beliefs. Fr Murphy suggested that the BP Guiding Association adopt the Ulster Flag, as it was more representative and inclusive. He felt that the uniform too was associated with the Protestant community and that a new neutral design would have to be created.[29] The tone of the memo suggests that it is unlikely that the proposals outlined by Fr Murphy to address the issues would ever be realised enabling successful integration.

Regardless of this, Guiding for Catholic Girls was simultaneously being developed mainly through clerical routes in Northern Ireland. In 1965 the Holy Trinity Guide Company was formed in Belfast. According to Noreen Conlon:

> I was fifteen and had lived in Turf Lodge for a year. While our city planners had supplied people with new homes, wide-open spaces and green fields there was [sic] no facilities for the young or old. No church, no schools, no youth club and no provisions of services at all, we had nowhere to go and nothing to do.[30]

The first meeting of the Holy Trinity Guides took place in Noreen's kitchen where she and her friend Eileen Doran set about training girls as patrol leaders. Initially they had no information on Guiding techniques so they consulted the

Baden Powell Handbook used by the Ulster Guide Association. With the assistance of their parish priest, Fr McKillop, the girls put the word out that a Catholic Guide Company was starting up in Turf Lodge. Noreen was astounded at the number of girls that turned up and the company soon had to search for a more appropriate premises for their meetings.

In the late 1960s Bishop William Philbin approached Moya Hinds, who was already well known for her youth work in Belfast, and asked her to assist with the development and formation of the Catholic Guides. With the help of three companions, Marie O'Hara, Josephine Friel and Nuala Moore, she formed companies in the Falls Road and other areas of Belfast before expanding into the areas of Derry and Down. Moya helped to incorporate an intensive training programme for leaders and spoke highly of the leaders involved in its development from the beginning. She stated that despite the troubles, relations with the Ulster Guide Association were good, although they did not take part in many mixed events. Relations were extremely good with the Ulster Boy Scouts who often shared their camping facilities with the Catholic Girl Guides.[31] In recognition of her work with youth in general in the North, Moya Hinds was awarded an MBE in the early 1980s. However, Moya made little of this award as she was afraid of reprisals by those who felt she shouldn't have accepted it. Guide units accommodated girls from Catholic families whose political views varied from moderate nationalists to hardline republican. Acceptance of an MBE award would have been seen by some as acceptance of the British regime in Ireland.

From 1969 Catholic Guide Units sprung up all over Northern Ireland, with seventeen in the Diocese of Down and Connor and five in Dromore.[32] There is no evidence to suggest that the Catholic Girl Guides in the North had political affiliations but the organisation was undoubtedly influenced by events at that time. Following the outbreak of violence after a civil rights march in Derry on 5 October 1968, the Catholic Girl Guides provided Catholic working-class girls with a chance to get out of the cities.

By the mid-1970s membership had grown dramatically. Catholic Guiding in the North at the time differed in many ways from the south and a letter dated 1975 to the Dublin Diocesan Commissioner, Sheila Redmond, from a company in the process of setting up in Armagh, demonstrates this:

> you do not appear to have a Campers badge, a Knotters badge or a Commonwealth Knowledge badge, this badge takes in having a knowledge of ten different commonwealth countries and collecting five different things each from a different Commonwealth country and keeping a scrap-book on the commonwealth and having a knowledge of the everyday living of a girl in one country and how it contrasts with ours ...[33]

If these badges were unavailable, the author of the letter intended to incorporate them into the Guiding programme in the North anyway, breaking away from the badge system in operation in the south. The author also wanted recognition in the form of a badge for Guides reaching a certain standard ... 'as for Queen's Guide ... we have decided to call it another name, National Guide perhaps. I am sure you have a copy of the Baden Powell Handbook, if not I will send you one.'[34] The author was unaware that a Commonwealth badge would not have applied in the south as the 26 counties of Ireland had been pronounced a republic in 1949, severing all connection with the United Kingdom.

Although there is only one letter of this kind on record, it is probably not completely off the mark to suggest that because of the political background and despite the religious segregation that existed in the North, there was more familiarity with the Ulster Guiding Association than with the southern Catholic one. Also, travel and communication between the Catholic Guides in the North with the south would have been extremely difficult, making the northern Guides more aware of the activities of the Ulster Girl Guides. The northern Guides differed from the south in other ways too: they referred to their companies as units; they incorporated camping under canvass before the south; and they had different coloured uniforms – green instead of brown.[35]

In order to bridge the divide between northern and southern Ireland, an organisation called Co-operation North was founded in 1979. Its founders hailed from the worlds of business, academic life, trade unions, professional bodies and voluntary organisations. Their aim was to promote goodwill and understanding between the people of Northern Ireland and the Republic. A variety of youth exchange programmes were organised through the 1980s that helped to break down cultural boundaries.

Federation

Meanwhile, the diocesan-based administration of the association allowed for each diocese to work independently, but this would soon change with federation. The initiative for a formal linking of the Guiding organisations in the various dioceses around the country appears to have begun in Cork where in 1971 efforts were made to bring Waterford, Wexford and Cork together for the purposes of training. The aim was to create uniformity of practice within the Catholic Guiding movement.

Cork also pointed out that there was a major difference between the two Guiding associations operating in the Republic. The Irish Girl Guides retained full membership of the World Association and benefited greatly from this, unlike the Catholic Girl Guides. A further matter which led to the establishment of a federation was that Cork had applied to the Department of Education for a grant and difficulties emerged in organising the distribution of such a grant amongst the various diocesan governing bodies.[36]

In 1972 the aims of a federation were outlined in a memorandum:

> The aim of the Federation of the Catholic Guides of Ireland shall be to foster Catholic Guiding in Ireland by bringing together for the purpose of mutual co-operation all Diocesan Catholic Girl Guide organisations not already affiliated to any national girl guide organisation.[37]

The Federation Committee consisted of representatives from all the dioceses who took part. A new badge and flag were designed representative of the Federation.

It was proposed that each diocese would have representation at national level while retaining complete autonomy. At this time there is evidence to suggest a distancing between the church and the Guides. Previously the chaplains would have been deeply involved in the administration of the organisation. It has been difficult to identify any particular reason for this other than, at this time, Irish society was generally moving towards a more secularised state. The Dublin guide chaplain, Fr Jim O'Sullivan, along with other diocesan chaplains supported a National Association but were not part of the negotiations that lead to its formation.[38] Also, evidence in the 1972 Federation memorandum showed that the role and influence of the chaplain at diocesan level was waning by the responsibility of spiritual guidance now being assigned to the captain/guider:

She is an educator in the same broad sense as parents are and when she appreciates this she sees the essentially religious content of her work.[39]

While previously this may have been taken for granted it was now officially acknowledged in writing.

It was proposed that a federation committee be formed to:

a) Administer the affairs of the Federation

b) Oversee the formation of a National Association

c) Act as an interim Executive Board when the Association was formed

d) Hold the first meeting of the National Council for the purpose of establishing the association and electing national officers, as well as transacting any other relevant business

e) Endeavour to obtain recognition of WAGGGS (World Association of Girl Guides and Girl Scouts)

f) Draw up rules for adoption at the National Council.[40]

Subsequently the Federation of Catholic Girl Guides of Ireland was formed. Visits and exchanges of information concerning aspects of Guiding between the dioceses followed.

The aim of forming a national association was soon realised, the administration of which operated at three different levels: national, diocesan or regional, and local.

The National Council was the governing body of the Association and would meet annually. At national level a National Commissioner, Secretary and Treasurer would be elected and a National Chaplain appointed. In 1977 the new Association was inaugurated at a mass held in St Mary's Pro-Cathedral, followed by a reception in Archbishop Byrne Hall.[41] The newly designed flag of the Association – the Cross of St Patrick on a white background with the Guide Badge surrounded by a scroll bearing the motto 'Courage, Fortitude and Readiness' on the centre – was presented to the first National Commissioner, Maureen Sloan, by Mr Fergus O'Brien TD, who represented the Minister for Education.

> Miss Maureen Sloan, Chairman of the Federation and first National Commissioner of the new body said that five years ago members of the various dioceses came together to explore the possibility of becoming a National Association again. The Federation was formed and a committee was set up to draw up a national constitution and rules.[42]

On 3 April 1977 the Federation of Catholic Girl Guides of Ireland officially became the Association of Catholic Guides of Ireland, dropping 'Girl' from the title and incorporating a national constitution.

The formation of the National Association represented a considerable step in the future organisation of the Catholic Guides.

The Way Forward

By this time the Catholic Guides of Ireland felt that they would be unable to develop their organisation effectively without membership of the World Association. As regular Guide activities continued Board members began to make tentative enquiries into how to obtain membership.

Ireland's entry into the EEC had, in general, created an acceptance of foreign cultures that made it easier for Guide and Scout groups to participate in events at an international level. The Jamborora of 1977 highlighted for the Catholic Guides the benefits of membership of the World Association. It was an international 'Camp of Friendship' to mark the Golden Jubilee of the foundation of the Catholic Boy Scouts of Ireland. The festival, held at the Cistercian Monastery of Mount Melleray in Co. Waterford, was opened by the President of Ireland, Dr Patrick Hillery. Approximately 12,000 Scouts and Guides from twenty-one countries took part. A range of events was planned including a twenty-four-hour hike through the Knockmealdown mountains and a spectacular fireworks display. Catholic Guides from local companies in Tramore and Waterford, as well as from around the country, attended the ten-day celebration and took part in a pageant re-enacting the ancient Fair of Tara and its legendary games. The festival was attended by many dignitaries, including Mrs Maureen Lynch, wife of an Taoiseach, Jack Lynch; the Right Rev. John Ward Armstrong, Church of Ireland Bishop of Waterford; and the Papal Nuncio, Rev. Dr Caetano Alibrandi, who presided at a concelebrated mass.[43]

For CBSI, the desire to be part of an international community of Scouts had led to a federation of the two Scouting associations in the Republic in 1965. This allowed CBSI members to participate in international events, which formerly had only been open to members of the Scout Association of Ireland. Since then both associations were entitled to full membership of the World Organisation of Scout Movements (WOSM).[44]

For Guides, there was a similar association. In the 1920s representatives of Girl Guide and Girl Scout organisations from various countries agreed to form the World Association of Girl Guides and Girl Scouts (WAGGGS). CGI's counterpart in the Republic of Ireland, the Irish Girl Guides (IGG), had held membership since its formation and represented the twenty-six counties at international events. In the northern counties, the Ulster Guides were represented at WAGGGS as part of the Girlguiding Association UK (GGUK).[45]

One of the reasons CGI had formed a Federation was because they felt that it would strengthen their position on application and provide them with an opportunity for membership of the World Association. In 1975 CGI approached WAGGGS regarding the possibility of obtaining membership. The consequences of this approach would result in intense negotiations between the two Guide movements, CGI and IGG, concerning representation at an international level.[46]

Cooperation between the Guide and Scout associations grew when, in May 1979, the centenary of the Apparition of Our Lady at Knock, Co. Mayo was celebrated. It was decided that there should be a joint celebration including all the Guide and Scout Associations in Ireland.

> Although this pilgrimage is a Catholic celebration it is not confined to Roman Catholic Guides/Scouts. The theme of the pilgrimage is 'Celebrating Together'.[47]

Papal Visit

Guides and Scouts coming together for different events was becoming the norm. In September 1979 Pope John Paul II visited Ireland and the various organisations assisted in the preparations and stewarding. There was extensive coverage of the event in all the national and local papers. The Catholic Guides played their part:

Guides to Present Silver Chalice.

The Catholic Guides of Ireland are presenting a chalice to Pope John Paul II. The National Commissioner, Maureen Sloan, handed it over to the Archbishop of Dublin, Dr Ryan at the

Archbishop's House, Drumcondra, Dublin for presentation to the Pope. It is made in Irish silver and the design has been inspired by the early eighth century Ardagh Chalice, now in the National Museum.[48]

Two million people welcomed the Pope to Ireland and the impact of his visit has been compared to the religious fervour on the occasion of the Eucharistic Congress.[49] Disruptions were caused to services including bus and rail, with new timetables being printed and published in national newspapers.[50] Security was tight and there was much concern for the Pope's safety following the recent Mountbatten murders.[51] Church bells rang out around the country as the Papal jet touched down at Dublin Airport.[52]

Hundreds of Guides from the Catholic Guides of Ireland and Irish Girl Guides associations volunteered to act as stewards in the Phoenix Park. There were strict instructions for stewards. Once on duty they came under the control of the Garda Síochána. Their duties were outlined as follows:

1. In every way possible to ensure the safety of the Holy Father
2. To assist the Gardaí in security, crowd control and other duties as required
3. To assist the public in every way possible for their comfort and safety.

Stewards were required to dress neatly and wear cap, sash and badge as provided. They were to keep passages and routes clear of loiterers at all times. During communion, stewards were asked to assist in making the ceremony run as smoothly as possible.

Two corrals close to the altar were reserved for the Catholic Guides, who invited the Irish Girl Guides and the Girls Brigade to join them. Three members of the Catholic Guides were selected to receive Holy Communion from the Pope, including the National Commissioner Maureen Sloan and two Brigini.[53]

The 1960s and 1970s represent a departure from the old to the new. The Catholic Guides of Ireland reflected prevailing attitudes throughout the period, culminating in the nationalisation of the organisation in 1977. This was a significant step and represented a watershed in the history of the association. Embracing a new modernity, like Ireland, the Catholic Guides would never be the same, and just as the nationalisation of the organisation represented a new beginning it also signalled the end of an era.

As the Catholic Guides of Ireland sought to gain membership of the World Association of Girl Guides and Girl Scouts (WAGGGS), negotiations were conducted during a period fraught with conflict. Irish society was rapidly changing: church control had become significantly diminished and there were calls for a more liberal social policy. Factions in Northern Ireland occupied a narrow gap between peace and violence. CGI, to a certain extent, reflected political conflicts concerning its members in the North and border recognition. Internally CGI was faced with creating a delicate balance between a modern, secular, voluntary association and an organisation that retained the ethos of the Catholic church, by which it was originally founded and administered.

Notes

1. Mary Robinson, President of Ireland, in Helen Exley, *In Celebration of Women: A Selection of Words and Paintings* (London, 1996)
2. Interview with Betty O'Donovan, CGI Head Office, Clanwilliam Terrace, 21 August 2008
3. *At Home with the Clearys*, documentary, RTE 1, screened 3 September 2007, 9.30 p.m.
4. Fr Brian D'Arcy, *A Different Journey* (Dublin, 2006) pp. 83–4
5. Catholic Guides of Ireland, Wexford 50th Anniversary Booklet 1995, Clanwilliam Terrace
6. Caroline McGuinness, Catholic Guides of Ireland, Wexford 50th Anniversary Booklet, Clanwilliam Terrace
7. Ibid.
8. Diarmaid Ferriter, *The Transformation of Ireland 1900–2000* (London, 2005) p. 597
9. *The Irish Times*, 14 September 1966
10. Diarmaid Ferriter, *The Transformation of Ireland 1900–2000* (London, 2005) p. 574
11. Ibid., p. 570

12. June Levine, *Sisters: The Personal Story of an Irish Feminist* (Dublin, 1982) pp. 92–3
13. In conversation with Dolores Farnan, Dublin, 23 May 2009
14. A. Coote and B. Campbell, *Sweet Freedom: The Struggle for Women's Liberation* (London, 1982) pp. 19–20
15. Arthur Marwick, *The Sixties:Cultural Revolution in Britain, France, Italy and the United States* (Oxford, 1998) p. 60
16. Walter Forde, 'The Aimless Rebellion', in *Christus Rex*, Vol., XXI, Number 1, January 1967
17. Barbara Goodall Wallace, *50th Anniversary Booklet: Catholic Guides of Ireland* (Wexford, 1995)
18. *Sunday Independent*, 24 November 1963
19. *Cork Examiner*, 9 May 1960
20. David Thornley, 'Ireland: End of an Era?' *Studies*, Volume 53, 1–17, spring 1964, p. 16
21. Diarmaid Ferriter, *The Transformation of Ireland, 1900–2000* (London, 2005) p. 557
22. *Evening Herald*, Monday, 2 July 1973
23. Sheila Redmond collection, CGI Archive, Clanwilliam Terrace (AB Ryan address)
24. Merit Badge Book, 1978, Sheila Redmond collection, CGI Archive, Clanwilliam Terrace
25. *Irish Independent*, 22 May 1978
26. Siobhan Kilfeather, 'Irish Feminism,' in *The Cambridge Companion to Modern Irish Culture* (eds) Joe Cleary and Claire Connolly (Cambridge, 2005) p. 108
27. Memorandum by Fr Padraig Murphy to Bishop Philbin 1966 referring to Catholic Guiding (1966) Down & Connor Diocesan Archive, Belfast
28. Ibid.
29. Memorandum unsigned and undated relating to Catholic Guiding (1966) Down & Connor Diocesan Archive, Belfast
30. Holy Trinity Guides 40th Anniversary Booklet 1996–2005, Clanwilliam Terrace

31. In conversation with Moya Hinds, Belfast, 26 May 2009
32. Guiders Link 1983, CGI Archive, Clanwilliam Terrace
33. Letter 4 February 1975, Sheila Redmond collection, CGI Archive, Clanwilliam Terrace
34. Ibid.
35. Interview, Marian Stewart and Máire McGrath, CGI, Belfast office
36. Letter to M. O'Kennedy, Federation file, 6 April 1971, Betty O'Donovan collection
37. Memorandum, CGI Archive, Clanwilliam Terrace
38. In conversation with Fr Jim O'Sullivan, Ballinteer, Dublin 30, September 2008
39. *The Role of the Adult in the Guide Section*, in an outline of the various roles played in the newly formed Federation, 1972, Federation file, CGI Archive, Clanwilliam Terrace
40. Memorandum of the Federation of Catholic Girl Guides of Ireland, Federation file, Clanwilliam Terrace
41. Information courtesy of Betty O'Donovan, Cork
42. *Cork Examiner*, Monday, 4 April 1977
43. Ibid.
44. www.scouts.ie
45. Brief History of Negotiations, CIGA Files 1980s–1990s, Clanwilliam Terrace
46. Ibid.
47. Joint Guide Scout Knock Committee, Maureen Sloan collection, HSA
48. *The Irish Times*, 26 September 1979
49. Diarmaid Ferriter, *The Transformation of Ireland 1900–2000* (London, 2005) p. 732
50. 'Timetable Alterations During Papal Visit to Ireland', Maureen Sloan collection, HSA

51. The Queen's cousin, Lord Louis Mountbatten, was assassinated in 1979 by the Provisional Irish Republican Army (IRA), who planted a bomb in his boat at Mullaghmore, County Sligo in the Republic of Ireland
52. *Evening Herald*, 25 September 1979
53. Papal Visit, Maureen Sloan collection, HSA

CHAPTER 5

GUIDING THROUGH UNCERTAIN TIMES:

CONNECTING WITH SECULARISM

1979–1993

Peace in your heart is where you begin,
so open it up and let sunshine in,
then open your mind and try and be fair,
even if people stand and stare,
the Peace in your heart can find a way,
to encourage others day by day,
to bring Peace to others must surely be,
always a top priority,
and a way of life for all to see.[1]

Through the 1980s

In the 1980s the Catholic Guides developed a new Guide programme, keeping pace with modern Irish life. Issues such as co-education and the secularisation of the state posed dilemmas for the organisation. With violence on the increase in the North, politicians sought to negotiate a peaceful resolution while at the same time, the Guides found themselves caught up in negotiations of their own concerning membership of the World Association that reflected historical and current political issues.

Seeking Membership of WAGGGS

The Jamborora of 1977 was just one event that highlighted for the Catholic Guides of Ireland the constraints on the organisation regarding development. The interaction between the other Scout/Guide organisations in the Republic with their international counterparts had been facilitated by their respective affiliations with World Scout/Guide associations.[2] The Jamborora had been an enormous success and showcased Scouting and Guiding in Ireland on the world stage. CGI felt they would be unable to grow if they were confined as a national organisation. Throughout the 1980s they actively sought a way to gain recognition by WAGGGS.

The worldwide Guiding movement has evolved over the years to meet societal needs but has retained essential elements such as the principle of voluntary membership, open to all without distinction of race, colour, creed or nation, and this has been reinforced in the constitution of the World Association. The Catholic Guides of Ireland needed to assess if their Guiding principles and techniques fitted with those of the World Association. By examining the general principles of Guiding as enunciated by the World Association for comparative purposes, CGI were satisfied they were eligible for membership.

The Principles of Guiding

One of the most familiar images of Guiding and Scouting was camping and the formation of a relationship with nature. The Guiding movement believed that:

> Living out of doors teaches the young person how to cope with the elements, to stand on her own feet, to be content with simple things. It also gives her the experience of silence, contemplation and harmony.[3]

The strong educational ethos incorporated into Guiding was aimed at the development of a 'whole person' able to transform society through the method of 'learning by doing' in the form of games, ventures and enterprises.

> It is in being placed in situations which demand an active response that the young are stimulated and inspired into action. The group is engaged all the time in the activities which are based on the interests and natural instincts of the girls – curiosity, love of adventure, the need to prove themselves.[4]

Guiding activities provided challenges for girls that in turn created a form of progressive self-training. The girls were impelled to train themselves in order to take part in a group and contribute to the success of projects. It was believed that progressive tests, where badges are earned to measure progress, can act as an incentive to learn. The challenges were met by the girls through teamwork in the form of the Patrol System, which consisted ideally of a group of six to eight girls, one of which is the leader, with each having an indispensable part to play in the group.

Symbolism too was seen by the Guiding movement as another powerful educational tool. Symbols such as the Guide salute, handclasp and uniform encouraged a sense of belonging and of personal communication that overcame the barriers of language, race and culture.

In Guiding, emphasis was placed on citizenship and the interaction between the Guides and the community in which they lived. In and through their activities Guides were encouraged to take part in community life – in local, national and international events. By doing so they came to understand fully their responsibilities as citizens.

> We are often confronted by the movement's poor public image ... In countries where the public image of Guiding is good, there is often a connection with the fact that the movement makes a real contribution to the development of the community.[5]

Negotiations

The Catholic Guides of Ireland believed that they embodied in their Guiding programme all the Guiding features of the World Association of Girl Guides and Girl Scouts. CGI felt that they would be able to contribute to and benefit from membership of such a prestigious international Guiding association. It was felt that membership would add credibility to the organisation along with other benefits such as:

- Belonging to a respected International Association
- Having access to International Training, European Seminars in order to share the experiences with our Association
- Allowing young people to be part of a World Community
- Developing mutual understanding among peoples through encouraging International Guide Friendships.[6]

In the mid-1970s the Catholic Guides of Ireland (CGI) were developing discussions between the Irish Girl Guides and WAGGGS. CGI first approached WAGGGS regarding the possibility of obtaining membership in December of 1975. WAGGGS informed them that the Irish Girl Guides were the recognised Irish national organisation and only one organisation from any one country could be recognised.[7]

In a subsequent letter from WAGGGS, dated June 1976, it was explained that membership could be permitted through a federation comprising several different Girl Guide and Girl Scout associations. Federation would allow the member associations to retain their separate identities. It was further suggested that another route to gaining membership would be to incorporate CGI within the structure of the Irish Girl Guides.

The letter outlined possible obstructions to world membership, such as the extent of clerical control of CGI. The WAGGGS constitution required a member organisation to be self-governing and non-denominational. Also, at that time, the CGI constitution made no reference to the international aspects of Guiding, a fundamental part of membership of WAGGGS.[8]

Having familiarised themselves with the rules concerning membership of WAGGGS the CGI approached the Irish Girl Guides (IGG) to negotiate a federation similar to that of the Boy Scouts.[9] IGG were reluctant, stating that 'Federation would be another dividing force in the country, whereas a single association would be a unifying force'.[10] At that time IGG were more in favour of a form of 'integration' rather than federation.[11] However, they agreed to meet with CGI to explore ways in which the two Guide organisations could work together. They also made it clear that they would only discuss matters relevant to the twenty-six counties.[12] A major obstacle for recognition at WAGGGS and for federation concerned the position of CGI in the North of Ireland. IGG was a twenty-six county organisation while CGI incorporated members from the whole island of Ireland. In 1980 it was estimated that CGI membership amounted to approximately 9,500 members in the Republic and 2,900 members in the North.

In May 1980 Maureen Sloan, National Commissioner, and Rita Daly, National Secretary, met with representatives of WAGGGS. At that meeting they made it clear that:

... at no time would they 'abandon' their units in Northern Ireland, nor would they enter into discussions of any kind that did not take account of these units ...[13]

In response to this, WAGGGS made it equally clear that it could only regard CGI as operating in two independent countries and that they would only be able to support discussion between CGI and IGG in relation to Guiding in the twenty-six counties. To complicate things further they felt that any reference to Guiding in the six counties of Northern Ireland would have to involve the Ulster Guiding Association and Girlguiding (UK).[14]

To avoid a deadlock, WAGGGS put forward proposals for talks between CGI and IGG to explore ways in which the two associations might join together. They suggested a six-member combined committee to define aims and objectives agreeable to both bodies but which should have the ultimate aim of establishing a movement for all Girl Guides in Ireland. In order to avoid exclusion of CGI members in the North it was also suggested that CGI include a representative from Northern Ireland on a separate internal committee 'to consider in detail all proposals for the joining together of the CGI and IGG' but who would not be included on the committee for negotiations between CGI and IGG.[15]

Regular meetings took place between the Catholic Guides of Ireland and the Irish Girl Guides with the aim of finding a way for CGI to become members of the World

Association of Girl Guides and Girl Scouts. The discussions explored ways and means of establishing closer co-operation between the two associations. In short, the problems were:

- The constitution and byelaws of WAGGGS recognised political boundaries
- WAGGGS could only recognise one national organisation in any one country.

The world bureau proposed that CGI and IGG establish a joint council enabling membership of WAGGGS to be shared by CGI and IGG on behalf of their members residing in the Republic of Ireland. WAGGGS agreed to allow members of CGI from the Republic to participate in international activities as representatives of a Joint Council excluding members from Northern Ireland.

Exclusion of northern members was still unacceptable to CGI and reaching a suitable compromise proved difficult. Talks between the two Irish Guiding organisations had reached a stale mate until 1987, when a breakthrough presented itself. A visit to Dublin in June of that year by Odile Bonte and Ellen Clarke of the World Association was arranged to propose the formation of a joint Council. [16]

It was concluded that with compromises on both sides it would be possible to form a Council incorporating a constitution that would enable both organisations to share membership of WAGGGS under certain conditions. Difficulties with CGI's constitution concerned the Guide promise. CGI agreed to change the text of this according to WAGGGS suggestions, making them more acceptable for inclusion.[17]

IGG concerns included the risk of involvement in a political situation vis-à-vis the North: they would not be able to incorporate CGI members in the North into their organisation in the Republic and this would, they felt, prevent progress towards a single movement. They also feared that if the joint Council failed they could lose their membership of WAGGGS. They expressed concern about the level of Catholic clerical control and interference in Guiding. They believed they were unfairly perceived as the 'Protestant' association in some quarters, despite the fact that they had 95 per cent Catholic membership. CGI allayed their fears, stating that the clerical influence within CGI was greatly overestimated. They stressed that whilst they were a Catholic association, they were in no way governed by the church. The task of the chaplains was to give spiritual and moral guidance as stated in their constitution:[18] 'CGI was open, had altered its constitution and did not discriminate against non-Catholics.'[19] Article 2 was amended in the CGI Constitution, officially ending governance of the Catholic Guide organisation by the Catholic church.[20] Although they maintained a devotional loyalty to the Catholic faith, CGI reflected social trends and had moved towards a more secular, voluntary organisation.

As a goodwill gesture CGI were invited by WAGGGS to attend the twenty-sixth World Guide Conference as observers in 1987. National Commissioner Bridie Dolan and National Treasurer Rita Daly attended the conference held in Egerton University College, Njoro, Kenya. The keynote speaker at the conference was Sally Kosgei, Kenya's new High Commissioner in London. She stressed the importance of building confidence in girls so they can be encouraged to take initiative:

> Women who have succeeded should pass on their skills and encourage other women to take their place in the world of tomorrow.[21]

Eventually negotiations reached conclusion, with IGG and CGI holding their first joint conference in the Radcliff Hall in Sandymount on 30 April 1988. Agreement had been reached and draft constitutions of the newly formed Joint Council of the Catholic Guides of Ireland and the Irish Girl Guides were formulated, outlining the aims and roles of both bodies. Information days were organised to keep members from each of the associations up to date on progress. In June 1989 an Extraordinary National Council Meeting was called and it was proposed by the National Executive Board of the Catholic Guides of Ireland that a Joint Council be established enabling membership of WAGGGS to be held by CGI and IGG on behalf of their members residing in the Republic of Ireland. It was resolved that all members of CGI could participate in the international activities of WAGGGS but only members residing in the Republic of Ireland could officially represent the Joint Council. CGI members in the North were given 'observer status'. This meant that they were able to attend Council meetings and participate in discussions but they would not be allowed to vote.[22]

Compromises had been made on both sides: IGG gave up their right to sole membership and accommodated CGI's request for recognition by WAGGGS. In turn CGI, believing Joint Council to be a 'stepping stone' to full recognition for all their members, made changes to their Constitution and agreed to a limited role for their northern members. In a final draft Constitution prepared for submission to WAGGGS for the Council of Irish Guiding Associations (CIGA), the fundamental principles were laid out as follows:

The Council of Irish Guiding Associations

a. accepts and adheres to the objects and the fundamental principles of the World Association of Girl Guides and Girl Scouts as contained in the Constitution and Bye-Laws of WAGGGS

b. has a membership which is:

    i. voluntary

    ii. open to all girls and young women without distinction of creed, race, nationality, or any other circumstance

c. is self governing, with freedom to formulate its policy and put it into practice

d. is independent of any political organisation and any political party.[23]

In July 1993 the Constitution was ratified by WAGGGS and the Catholic Guides of Ireland in the Republic gained full membership, excluding members in Northern Ireland.

Guide Leaders

Problems recruiting suitable leaders were still an issue for the organisation and at Parents' Day in the Iveagh Gardens in June 1980 an appeal was made for girls to come forward and lead new Guide companies in many of the new residential areas around Dublin.[24] In 1981 a headline in the *Irish Independent* stated, 'Wedding bells tolling trouble for the Irish Catholic Guides':

> The trip to the altar is taking a toll on Ireland's Girl Guides. Too many girls are marrying and throwing their brown uniforms out of the window. The Catholic Guides of Ireland is suffering from a lack of officers, a shortage which has led to the organisation's public relations officer, May Garvan, to appeal to past members to come back and help.[25]

May stated she would like past members who have married and taken care of their children to return to the organisation where they would be made senior officers.[26]

Development

In 1982 Bridie Dolan was appointed National Commissioner for the Catholic Guides of Ireland. In that year she launched the new Guide newsletter, Guiders Link and the new modernised Guide programme, Climb Every Mountain. The new programme inculcated a sense of achievement. Awards for Brigin Guide were named after mountains in Ireland, such as Errigal and Carrantuohill, and awards for Guides were named after European mountains. For Ranger Guides the highest award was called Everest. The challenges centred on preparation, training, participation and achievement. Beginning at the Lend a Hand programme for Brigini, a Guide then progressed to the Come Guiding programme and then on to the Rangers Way programme. Handbooks were prepared for each section and, on the 2 November 1982, the Minister of State at the Department of Education, Maire Geoghegan Quinn, launched the programme. She stated:

> It embodies the team spirit of Guiding that makes the ultimate goals of personal development and formation achievable in a group context ... you have developed a high level of professionalism as educators in this respect.[27]

Quinn also acknowledged the work of the Catholic Guides of Ireland as a volunteer organisation and commended the high level of commitment needed to produce such an effective Guiding service.

As CGI negotiated for recognition by WAGGGS, other issues presented problems for the organisation. A drop in membership, particularly among the older girls, was a major problem. It was felt that the organisation would benefit from definitive objectives and priorities in the areas of development, training, communication, structure and management. A contributory factor to this drop in membership was the rise in popularity of mixed youth organisations. The government supported a co-educational policy and CGI felt under pressure to comply with this trend in order to avoid a conservative image.

In 1986 representatives from the Catholic Boy Scouts of Ireland approached CGI to discuss the establishment of mixed scouting units. This provoked debate within the organisation focussed on two main areas:

1. CGI's policy on single-sex organisations and their relevance in modern Ireland
2. Effects of mixed scouting on CGI membership.[28]

Overall, CGI felt that single-sex organisations were of benefit to girls because they gave girls and young women an opportunity to take on responsibilities that they were unable to do within a mixed association. It was considered that girls and young women would have more opportunity for personal and social development in a female setting. Being part of an all-female group, girls and young women would have more opportunity:

- To make decisions on their own
- To work in teams and to negotiate on an equal basis
- To assert themselves
- To develop a sense of identity and self worth
- To see other women in positions of responsibility.[29]

On the other hand it was felt that Guiding and Scouting working together would have more to offer than separate programmes. In a discussion document on the matter it was stated:

> The trend in today's world is towards the bringing together of boys and girls both for formal education and for out of school activities. Co-education aims to break down barriers between the sexes, to do away with stereotyped sex roles and to help build better relationships between boys and girls. As a youth organisation CGI needs to become aware of this development and to look at ways of responding to it.[30]

After much consideration it was felt that a broad co-educational programme would be desirable.[31] Through the 1980s there is evidence of more interaction with other

Guide/Scout movements such as the formation of a Joint Committee between the Catholic Boy Scouts of Ireland, the Irish Girl Guides, the Scout Association of Ireland and the Catholic Guides of Ireland to examine a programme of rules for Safety Out of Doors.[32]

From a social perspective too, Camps such as Waterwise '88 provided an opportunity for Ranger Guides to socialise at mixed discos and ceilis. Fifty Ranger Guides along with guests from the other Guide and Scout organisations took part in a fun-filled, water-based activity camp. The weekend took place in Dromineer on the banks of the Shannon. Two barges were moored side by side to provide accommodation and various outdoor events were organised during the day, with barbecues, discos and céilís arranged for the evening.[33]

The Smythe Cup held in Inistioge in Co. Kilkenny in 1989 was another mixed Guide/Scout event and provided an opportunity for Guides to show off their skills. One of the challenges presented to St Brendan's Guide Company from Cork was to build a raft. One Guide recalled:

> We were given a picture and we had to copy it to a 'T' with the equipment given. We finished the raft in no time but we hadn't completed the full task. We had to make sure our raft would float so we tested it. Four from our patrol paddled the raft over to the other side of the river singing 'Row, Row, Row Your Boat'.[34]

Since the formation of the National Association in 1977, CGI had rented offices to accommodate the new administration. In August 1987 a more permanent arrangement was made with the purchase of a premises at 12 Clanwilliam Terrace, Grand Canal Quay in Dublin. 'The event marked a milestone in the development of the Association after 10 years in rented accommodation.'[35]

> This will provide a permanent National base and make our work of administering the Association easier and more efficient. It will also be more cost effective in the long term when the ten year mortgage is repaid.[36]

Troubled Times

At this time, 1980s, Ireland was suffering from what Terence Browne described as 'a lack of self-image after the economic and social changes of the 1960s and 1970s. Gone was the version of the national identity of Ireland as Gaelic, Catholic and Republican'.[37] Guiding in the North continued to grow. New companies formed in the diocese of Dromore provided girls with much-needed relief from the constant unrest. Violence between Nationalist and Unionist factions in Northern Ireland was on the increase. The early 1980s saw the opening of dialogue between the British and Irish governments that culminated in the Anglo-Irish Agreement signed at Hillsborough Castle on 15 November 1985. The Agreement gave the Irish government a consultative role in aspects of governance in Northern Ireland.[38] Significantly, Britain declared it would not stand in the way of a United Ireland if, in the future, the majority in the North desired it.[39] Unionists marched in protest at the Agreement. There was a perception by northern Protestants that law in the Republic was influenced by Roman Catholic social policy, and they feared that their civil and religious liberties would not survive in a United Ireland in which Roman Catholicism would be the religion of the majority.[40]

Hunger strikes by Provisional Irish Republican Army prisoners in the early 1980s had raised nationalist sympathy and support grew in favour of the political wing of the IRA, Sinn Féin, who successfully contested Northern elections. Highlighted was the inequality between Catholics and Protestants, particularly in the workforce in the North. In 1985 Tom King, the Northern Ireland Secretary, announced a 'fair employment' policy for Northern Ireland threatening firms that discriminated against people for their religious beliefs with financial sanctions including the withdrawal of government grants.[41]

CGI participated in events aimed at countering violence and encouraging peace. In fact it could be said that the overriding theme of the 1980s was peace. The Festival for Youth was held at the King's Hall in Belfast in 1983 and youth organisations from around the country attended, including CGI. The aim of the festival was to 'pave the way to a better future for the young people of Northern Ireland'.[42] For National Peace Day, 2 October 1983, a booklet of prose and poetry was published containing the works of members of CGI north and south and given to the Papal Nuncio, Dr Gaetano Alibrandi for presentation to Pope John Paul II in Rome. CGI took part in many activities 'designed to create a greater awareness of the need for peace in our lives and the community in general'.[43]

War and Peace
Peace is such a beautiful thing,
Just think of all the happiness it brings,
Peace makes people laugh with joy,
But only war makes people cry.
With longings for peace to come,
And unite our people and countries as one.

During war, all people long,
With weary hearts and tearful song,
That this war will come to an end,
And peace will reign here once again.
They pray that their children will never know,
The horrors of war that has been so.[44]

These were difficult times for Guiding in Northern Ireland. With the support of the priests in the parish, the Holy Trinity Guide Company in the Turf Lodge area of Belfast had acquired a new den. Josephine Higgins recalled:

> One night I had a group of Guides in the Den and a blast bomb went off outside. I couldn't get them out so we had to wait for the police to come to take us out. I had to take each of them home because there was no way of contacting the parents.[45]

Other Guide leaders in the North recalled how parents were sometimes reluctant to let their daughters travel to Guide meetings in winter as they sometimes ran into camouflaged army foot patrols:

Leaders used to meet everybody at the shops at a certain time and then we would all travel to the Guide meeting together for safety reasons. If we were travelling on buses to Guide events we would get the girls to take off their neckerchiefs because you didn't know what kind of areas we would be going through. We didn't want to give in to intimidation. Looking back, the Guides was probably the only thing that kept us sane as young people.[46]

Catholic Guides in the North participated in many cross-community events to help bridge the divide and create dialogue between the communities but even these events sometimes proved divisive. Josephine Higgins recalled an incident at an event held at City Hall, Belfast where youth groups representing both communities gathered to receive a certificate of peace from the Lord Mayor:

Carol Ewings was our Diocesan Commissioner and she went up to collect our certificate on our behalf. You'd want to have heard the boos in the hall when they mentioned Catholic Guides. It was children doing it, not adults, but you were still up against discrimination because you were Catholic.[47]

However, the happy memories of Guiding in the North far outweighed any negative ones. St Paul's Guide Unit was formed in 1967 in Colinpark Street in Belfast.

We had a fantastic parent's committee, they worked really hard for us. We put on shows and pantomimes,

Cinderella and Ali Baba. We felt like movie stars in the costumes the committee had made for us. St Paul's hall in Hawthorne Street was packed and we were even in the Irish News. Right through the uncertain times of the troubles, St Paul's Guides was a haven for many young girls.[48]

Like their southern counterparts, camping prior to the 1970s took place in suitable accommodation in the countryside. Sharon Devlin remembers one trip to Kilmore House in Glenariffe:

That spooky house in the middle of the Glens of Antrim. Lights went off, gas cookers turned off and came back on again with no explanation. All the girls were in the living room with the fire glowing in the grate. Party time and singing songs was the order of the night. The leaders were peeling potatoes, cutting onions and cooking mince steak. Suddenly there was a gust of wind and the lights went out. You can imagine the squeals![49]

Relations with the Church

In the south there was a growing acceptance of the secularlisation of the state. The fifth amendment of the Constitution Act of 1972 had removed the special position of the Catholic church from within the Irish state.[50] Criticism of the church centred on issues relating to divorce, contraception

St Peter's Basillica, Rome, 1950

Guide performance of *The Gondoliers*, 1957

The Dining Car, Redbarn, Cork, 1946

Parents' Day, Iveagh Gardens, 1959

Raising the Flag, Fernhill, 1960

Parents' Day at the Mardyke, Cork, 1960s
(May Dowling collection)

Guide outing, 1960s
(Catherine Lenihan collection)

President John F. Kennedy visits Ireland, 1963
(photographer unknown)

Pilgrimage to Rome, 1960 (Catherine Lenihan collection)

Guides on an outing, Northern Ireland, 1970s
(Marian Stewart collection)

Northern Ireland Catholic Guides, Jamborora 1977,
(Marian Stewart collection)

National Council Committee, 1977

Outdoor skills

Guides at Phoenix Park during visit of
Pope John Paul II, 1979

At Jamborora 1977
*from left: Brid Galvin, Joanne Travers, Gaye Gavin, Paula Sheedy,
Patricia Kennealy, Aine McCarthy, Maureen Fitzgerald and
Paula Lardner. Paula Brackenbury collection, CGI archive (Waterford),
Clanwilliam Terrace*

Maureen Sloan and Brigin receiving Communion
from Pope John Paul 11, 1979

President Patrick Hillery being greeted by Guides
at the opening of Aonach 1985

Waterwise 1988, 'Shannon Sailing'

Participants, Smythe Cup, 1989

Larch Hill Guide Camp, 1988

Guide Badges, 1980s

Parent's Day, Iveagh Gardens, Dublin, 1980s
(photographer unknown)

New Catholic Guide Headquarters, Cork

Event organised for children of Chernobyl in Cork, 1991

Cooking at camp, 1980s

Trip to Jersey, 1998

Official launch of CHOICES, the new Guide programme,
19 February 2006

and abortion with what Fine Gael leader, Garret Fitzgerald, referred to as their 'irrationality' on such matters.[51] Despite this, thousands flocked to a grotto in Ballinspittle in Cork in 1985 where moving statues and reports of miracles reflected perhaps a poignant need for religious belief at a time of violence and uncertainty.[52]

As can be seen from the negotiations concerning world membership, CGI had made it clear that the Catholic church no longer had governance in any aspect of the organisation. However, the Catholic ethos of the Catholic Guides of Ireland remained strong. In May 1983 at a commissioning of CGI officers in the Pro-Cathedral in Dublin, they 'promised to do their best for the spiritual and temporal welfare of all members of the Catholic Guides of Ireland'.[53] Demonstrations of faith were displayed within the organisation too, such as the pilgrimage to Faughart, Co. Louth, the birthplace of St Brigid, in which 600 members from the Diocese of Armagh took part. Another included 390 members of CGI who took part in a pilgrimage to Knock. Past members of CGI raised funds to send Guides on pilgrimage to Lourdes, where they helped with the sick and invalids.

Guiding in the Community

Guiding really was for everybody and accommodated girls with disabilities. Catholic Guide companies such as Buíon[54] Vincent, on the Navan Road, Dublin, included mentally disabled girls attached to St Vincent's residential school. The aim of the company was to encourage the children to integrate and mix socially. The Guide programme was adapted to their needs and members were helped and encouraged to take part in all activities. Buíon Lucy was a Brigin company attached to St Mary's school for the blind in Dublin. The company's handbook was translated into braille with the help of the governor and men of Arbour Hill prison. Other companies around the country also adapted their programmes to accommodate disabled Guides.[55] Integration and acceptance of all was very much in keeping with the Guide principles of openness and service to the community.

In 1985, International Youth Year, Dr Patrick Hillery, President of Ireland established the President's Awards for personal excellence, achievement and voluntary service. Participants could earn a bronze, silver or gold award under headings such as:

- Community involvement
- Personal skills
- Physical recreation
- Venture projects.[56]

Also in that year, Aonach ('Fair') '85 was launched by the President. The event promised to be a fun-filled, action-packed activity weekend based on the themes of International Youth Year – participation, development and peace.[57] Including children from communities all around the country helped foster a sense of belonging and contributed to a feeling of unity, essential in a national association.

To mark their diamond jubilee fiftieth anniversary, CGI celebrations in 1988 included 'Friendship Camps' for Guides and Brigin Guides. The first national Brigin Camp held over a weekend in August was attended by 350 Brigini from all over Ireland.

The event took place at the King's Hospital School in Palmerstown with an array of activities including swimming, ten-pin bowling, treasure hunts and disco dancing. Ten of the Brigin Guides were interviewed on the popular RTÉ radio programme *Pop-a-rama*, which dedicated the whole show to the event. Older Guides had their week-long national camp in Larch Hill attended by approximately 200 members from six dioceses. They had an equally impressive choice of events to participate in, including archery, ice-skating and an assault course.[58]

A nuclear accident at Chernobyl on 26 August 1986 was a catastrophe for the people of the area and an ecological and social calamity on a global scale. Nuclear contamination affected 2.2 million people and destroyed 20 per cent of the total farmland and 15 per cent of the forest. The disaster necessitated the implementation of a major resettlement programme for the people of the area. In 1991 the Catholic Guides of Ireland, together with the other three Guide and Scout associations, IGG, CBSI and SAI, were host to 40 young people from the affected region. The aim of the project was to provide holidays for 1,000 young people. Priority was given to orphans, children abandoned by their parents and to children in large families. The Russian visitors spent time at camps all over Ireland and local communities rallied to their aid with all kinds of generous donations. Shops and businesses provided food and clothes, and the provision of a coach assisted with travel.[59] It was reported in the *Evening Herald* that the children enjoyed Irish food most of all:

> The children many of whom are orphaned and abandoned, all live within 40km of Chernobyl and their towns have been hit by radioactive contamination, forcing them to boil foods, especially fresh vegetables.[60]

In 1989 the CGI Young Women's Project was launched. The event took place in Neilstown, Dublin over sixteen weeks from February to May. Girls aged 14 to 16 who had left the school system and were unemployed could take part in a selection of classes run by the Guides. The classes were diverse and covered areas such as cookery, crafts, hairdressing, horse riding, hiking and aerobics. It was hoped to expand community projects like this to areas outside of Dublin.[61]

Throughout the 1980s CGI were obliged to adapt to a fast-changing Irish society. While retaining a Catholic ethos the organisation severed all connection with the Catholic church regarding governance. A new Guide programme and magazine modernised their image and recognition by the World Association gave CGI the credibility they sought. Unfortunately, World membership still excluded members in the North. Against the background of political division and violence, CGI would continue to seek inclusion for them into the twenty-first century. However, the speed with which Irish society was changing would pose ongoing difficulties for CGI. Further challenges lay ahead: the Celtic Tiger representative of Ireland's economic boom would prove to have disastrous consequences for CGI, as they attempted to develop a fresh, modern image to attract new members. Negotiations continued as CGI tried to acquire recognition by WAGGGS for their northern members, the conclusion of which represents a new beginning.

Notes

1. A. Trimby. Collection of Poems on the Theme of Peace, 1984, compiled by the Catholic Guides of Ireland
2. Other organisations in the Republic included the Irish Girl Guides who represented Ireland at the World Association of Girl Guides and Girl Scouts (see Chapter 1). The Catholic Boy Scouts of Ireland and the Scout Association of Ireland had formed a Federation in 1965, so both organisations would have representation at the World Organisation of Scout Movements. The Scout Association of Ireland was formerly known as the Boy Scouts of Ireland. In 1968, reference to the word 'Boy' was removed from the title to open the way for the admission of girls. (See www.scouts.ie)

3. Beryl Cozens-Hardy, *The Essential Elements of Girl Guiding/Girl Scouting* (London, 1975/82)
4. Ibid.
5. Ibid.
6. Working Towards World Membership, CGI Archives, Clanwilliam Terrace, Dublin 2
7. Letter from WAGGGS, 7 January 1976, signed Lyn Joynt, CIGA files, Clanwilliam Terrace
8. Letter from WAGGGS to IGG, 17 June 1976, copy CGI, CIGA files, Clanwilliam Terrace
9. A.J. Gaughan, *Scouting in Ireland*, Dublin 2006
10. Letter from IGG, 18 November 1976, CIGA files, Clanwilliam Terrace
11. Report of meeting between representatives of CGI & World Bureau, 17 May 1980, CIGA files, Clanwilliam Terrace
12. Letter from IGG, 18 November 1976, CIGA files, Clanwilliam Terrace
13. Report of meeting between representatives of CGI & World Bureau, 17 May 1980, CIGA files, Clanwilliam Terrace
14. Ibid.
15. Ibid.
16. Report on visit made by Odile Bonte and Ellen Clarke on behalf of World Bureau, 2–3 June 1987, CGI Archives, Clanwilliam Terrace
17. Report of meeting with representatives of CGI and WAGGGS, 17 May 1980, CGI Archive, Clanwilliam Terrace
18. Ibid.
19. Minutes of a meeting between WAGGGS, CGI and IGG, September 1989, CGI Archive, Clanwilliam Terrace
20. Minutes of National Council meeting, 1986, Betty Donovan collection
21. Guiders Link 1987
22. Letter to Ellen Clark, WAGGGS, 12 June 1989, CGI Archives, Clanwilliam Terrace
23. CIGA Constitution draft for WAGGGS July 1992, CGI Archives, Clanwilliam Terrace

24. *Irish Independent*, Monday, 30 June 1980
25. Ibid., Monday, 18 May 1981
26. Ibid., Monday, 18 May 1981
27. Guiders Link 1982, Catholic Guides of Ireland newsletter
28. National Executive Board Minutes 1986, CGI Archive, Clanwilliam Terrace
29. CGI Guiders Handbook, Clanwilliam Terrace
30. *Facing the Future*, Co-Education and Guiding, Discussion Document, National Council Meeting, 28 March 1987, Sheila Redmond Collection
31. National Executive Board Minutes 1986, CGI Archive, Clanwilliam Terrace
32. Guiders Link 1987/88
33. Ibid.
34. Guide Memories of Smythe Cup 1989, May Dowling collection, Cork
35. In conversation with Dolores Farnan, 21 May 2009
36. Catholic Guides of Ireland Report, 1987
37. Terence Browne, p. 319
38. Tim Pat Coogan, *Disillusioned Decades: Ireland 1966–1987* (Dublin, 1987)
39. Terence Brown, *Ireland: A Social and Cultural History 1922–2002* (London, 2004) pp. 334–5
40. Ibid.
41. Tony Gray, *Ireland this Century* (London, 1994) p. 321
42. Guiders Link 1983, Catholic Guides of Ireland newsletter
43. Minutes of National Council Meeting 1983
44. Deborah Byrne, Collection of Poems on the Theme of Peace, 1984, compiled by the Catholic Guides of Ireland
45. Interview with Josephine Higgins, Belfast, 21 February 2009
46. Group interview, CGI Belfast, 21 February 2009
47. Interview with Josephine Higgins, Belfast, 21 February 2009
48. Deirdre McKibbin, Memories of Guiding, St Paul's Girl Guide Unit, 1967–2007, courtesy of Sharon Devlin, Belfast
49. Sharon Devlin, Memories of Guiding, St Paul's Girl Guides, 1967–2007, Belfast

50. Alvin Jackson, *Ireland 1798–1998* (London, 2003) p. 395
51. Dermot Ferriter, *The Transformation of Ireland, 1900–2000* (London, 2005) p. 735
52. Guiders Link 1983, CGI Archive, Clanwilliam Terrace
53. Diarmuid Ferriter, *The Transformation of Ireland 1900–2000* (London, 2004) p. 735
54. Irish word. Exact meaning: band, gang, group. In this case it refers to a Guide company
55. Guiders Link 1983, Catholic Guides of Ireland Newsletter
56. Guiders Link 1985, Catholic Guides of Ireland Newsletter
57. Minutes National Council meeting March 1985
58. Guiders Link autumn 1988
59. *Evening Echo*, 18 July 1991
60. *Evening Herald*, 27 July 1990
61. Guiders Link 1989/90, CGI Archive

CHAPTER 6

ONWARDS AND UPWARDS:

DIFFERENT IRELAND; DIFFERENT GIRL GUIDES

1993–2009

❧❧

*We seek somehow to communicate to every person
who lives here that we want for all of your
children the right to grow up in an Ireland
where this entire island gives every man and woman
the right to live up to the fullest of their God-given
abilities, and gives people the right to live
in equality, freedom and dignity.*[1]

Ireland in the 1980s had suffered from an economic
downturn resulting in increased emigration. The 'Brain
Drain' was the term used to refer to the thousands of
well-educated young people who left the country in
search of employment. This was in complete contrast to
the 'Celtic Tiger' of the 1990s, a period in which Ireland
experienced unprecedented economic success and full
employment. According to David McWilliams, 'the
1990s gave birth to a very different Ireland. The

experience of being Irish for the young people of the 90s was very different from past generations. The emigration of the previous decade had passed them by. They were the product of full employment and wealth in a new Ireland'.[2]

New Image

Reflecting the new Ireland, the early 1990s saw CGI adopt a change of image. It was felt a new style of uniform would present a more modern look and help attract new members. A graduate from the National College of Art and Design was given responsibility for the design of the new uniform, which was unveiled on RTÉ television's *Head to Toe* fashion programme. The *Irish Independent* reported:

> Out went the mud brown dull shade and in came a striking turquoise teal which is teamed up with either the lemon polo tee-shirt or the paler blue cotton blouse.[3]

Commenting on CGI's new look a Guide spokesperson stated:

> ... the ethos of the Girl Guides has changed dramatically over the years and it's a much more liberal association in both thought and outlook. Irish Archbishops felt camping wasn't suitable for girls while the Boy Scouts were free to pitch their tents ... Girl Guides are now free from this type of ... repression and hike off for weekends at the drop of a

neckerchief ... the Girl Guides are multi-denominational too, even though the word 'Catholic' is still incorporated into the title.[4]

The spokesperson felt that the Guides was a great place to meet and make friends: 'it's also completely classless and politically well-balanced. It brings children together from all over the country and lets them network and really mix with each other.'[5] CGI were anxious to promote a liberated, modern organisation and it was intended that this philosophy be reflected in the new Guide uniform. However, there were many changes to the style of uniform before agreement was eventually reached.

At the same time as deliberations were taking place concerning the new uniform, a new logo was introduced. A combination of symbols was suggested to promote a 'progressive youth organisation in touch with the wants of the modern teenager'.[6] A design agency was asked to prepare a logo that would 'combine a sense of organisation and regiment, a sense of tradition and a sense of the spirit of youth and vitality that is indigenous to CGI'. The following elements were incorporated into the design:

- *The Compass*: suggestive of the outdoors and adventure as well as stressing other aspects such as precision and direction. This is an international symbol.
- *Internal Loop and Arrow*: gives the feeling of looking to the future, speed and inspiration. There is also the benefit that

this resembles the internationally recognised symbol for recycling, which is a worthy trait of any organisation.

*   *The Triangle*: This is a symbol of strength and tradition, and gives a sense of heraldry. It could be interpreted as representing the Holy Trinity, which is entirely appropriate to the origins of CGI. It also suggests protection and therefore comfort.

It was intended to use the logo in all matters relating to the public, i.e. books, press releases and other printed material, and it was included on the newly designed uniform.[7]

The children members of CGI were now divided into four categories: Cygnets aged 5–6 years, Brigini, aged 6–11 years, Guides aged 10–17 years and Rangers aged 15–19 years. A survey carried out in 1999 by UCD Smurfit School of Business found that the current programme was inadequate and that some aspects were considered too childish or old fashioned.[8] Girls in the Cygnet, Brigin and Guide categories were most satisfied with the programme but girls in the Ranger category cited unstructured meetings, mixing with younger Guides, being responsible for younger girls and a lack of leadership as reasons for dissatisfaction. However, the outdoor activities such as camping, mountaineering and hiking were still extremely popular.

The Ranger Guides also expressed a desire to receive more responsibility and input into decisions and activities.[9] The formation of a Members Council would allow for the girls to take a more active role in the organisation and provide a chance to get together and look at areas of

Guiding that might need to change.[10] It was agreed that there was a need for a new programme handbook that would have a modern, user-friendly format that would take the organisation into the twenty-first century with information technology mixing with the traditional Guide skills such as campcraft. The changes took place under four main headings: programme, structure, events and out of doors. Committees were formed to look at all these areas and how best to update and improve them.

Choices

After several years of planning and debate, on 19 February 2006 the official launch of the new Guide programme took place. Taking into consideration the findings of the survey carried out by the Smurfit School of Business in 1999, the new CHOICES programme intended to stretch the skills of Guides in a range of areas including health, communication and the environment.[11] Five-hundred girls from all around the country released five-hundred balloons en masse into the sky over Dublin with the event launched by the Lord Mayor of Dublin, Cllr Catherine Byrne, and Minister for Education, Mary Hanaffin.[12]

Tackling Youth Issues through Guiding

In the 1990s an increased emphasis on youth culture witnessed the rise of boy bands, with U2 and The Corrs already established superstars. Television, DVD and computer games became popular forms of home entertainment for young people, testimony to the new wealth permeating Irish society. The increased demand on television for light entertainment and news saw the launch of two new Irish television channels in the 1990s, TG4 and TV3, while familiar style news and entertainment in the form of the Irish Press collapsed in 1995.[13]

These popular forms of static entertainment have been held partially responsible for the more sedentary way of life adopted by young people, which has led to an increase in obesity and the generally unhealthy lifestyles of Irish children.[14] A National Youth Health Programme Report undertaken by the National Task Force on Obesity (2004) found that in a survey of Dublin schoolgirls, 20 per cent were taking up smoking or continuing to smoke as a weight-loss strategy. The World Health Organisation also reported that it had serious concerns about the increasing consumption of sweetened carbonated drinks as a contributory factor to the obesity epidemic. In response to this the Department of Health and Children provided guidelines on nutrition for primary schools and pre-schools, with a greater emphasis on the importance of play in child development and physical well-being.[15] It is considered that children who spend more time participating in physical activity have a reduced risk of becoming overweight.

CGI played an important role in tackling these issues. As already outlined in a previous chapter, the outdoor education programme was a fundamental part of

Guiding. These activities provided opportunities for self-development; for learning to live together; for leadership and character development; for developing physical and mental strength and endurance; and for enjoyment and satisfaction.[16]

Less Church Involvement

From the start the Catholic church had played a formative and dominant role in the organisation. However, by the twenty-first century this position had weakened considerably. It could be said that the spiritual aspect of the organisation was now pursued independently. Some members of CGI express regret at what they perceive as the church's abandonment of them and the distancing of the local chaplains who had once played an important role in the spiritual direction of the organisation.[17] However, the church could lay equal claim to being abandoned by CGI because of its association with old-fashioned ideas. Currently a National Chaplain is appointed to CGI by the hierarchy to act as spiritual advisor to the Guides. However, due to a fall in the number of priests and increasing demands on his time, his involvement in Guide activities is minimal. On a local level, where once enrolment ceremonies were carried out by the local chaplain, it is now more often carried out by a Commissioner or Guider/captain.[18]

Through the 1990s, CGI together with all institutions dealing with children were made increasingly aware of the dangers posed to children through child abuse. Clerical abuse was not unique to Ireland but in a country where the Catholic church, since the foundation of the state, dominated in the areas of health, education and social teaching, the widespread sense of hurt, loss of faith and respect for the church was devastating.[19] There was an awareness across all organisations – religious and lay – that there was a need to put in place clear child protection procedures. CGI sought advice and direction from other youth organisations and voluntary child-care agencies in developing a suitable child protection policy. The aim of the policy was to protect both children and the volunteers who worked with them. For children the policy recommended that at company meetings:

> Three leaders be present for the duration of company meetings with the exception of Cygnet Guide companies, which should have a minimum of three, plus one leader to every five Cygnet Guides. The following adult/child ratio applies:
>
> Cygnet Guides 1:5 (always)
> Brigin Guides 1:8 (Outdoor 1:6)
> Guides 1:10
> Ranger Guides [N/A]

All leaders were assigned a reporting officer to whom they reported when child protection issues arose. General procedures for leaders were as follows:

DO

Be observant
Be aware of your responsibilities as a leader
Keep an incident/accident book
Ensure adequate supervision at all times
Listen and believe
Follow the reporting procedures

DO NOT

Promise to keep secrets
Permit bullying
Allow inappropriate physical contact

TRAINING

All leaders will be obliged to undertake child protection
training as part of their basic course and such training
should be updated and renewed as required.

The policy also aimed to protect leaders:

> As well as offering our leaders good practice
> guidelines in their work with young people, this
> policy is also designed to affirm and encourage
> those who give their time and skills in this
> organisation and recommends guidelines that will
> reinforce good practice and help to identify and
> counteract bad practice. In the case of abuse
> occurring in an organisation, the abuse not only
> causes hurt to the children but undermines the

integrity and the calling of the vast majority who conscientiously care about children and their well being.[20]

Within CGI an intensive training programme for leaders had always been necessary before a leader could be placed in charge of a company. This involved the completion of a course in first aid, with a certificate awarded either by the Red Cross, the Order of Malta, St Johns Ambulance or the Civil Defence. Other areas of training for leaders included problem solving, substance abuse and programme planning. The camping policy of CGI states that leaders who run Guide camps need to hold an appropriate qualification of the organisation and each camping event must also have the appropriate insurance cover.[21]

The child protection policy provided direction for leaders in circumstances such as child abuse and its prevention, good standards of practice and recruitment, and vetting of volunteers. Clearly child protection was essential but the necessity to provide a policy signalled the end of the seemingly innocent carefree days of Guiding of the past.

For some members of CGI, less church involvement evoked much sadness. The church successfully organised and facilitated the building of an enormously popular Guide movement for young girls. The chaplains who once were very involved – organising pilgrimages and performing religious/Guide ceremonies – were no longer a feature of the organisation in the way they had been. However, the Guide organisation still retains a Catholic ethos in respect of its origins.

The Northern Situation and WAGGGS

As CGI focussed on their new image they also began to weigh up the necessity of pursuing full membership of WAGGGS for their members in the North of Ireland. At the National Executive Board meeting in November 1994 the northern members present were asked if they wanted to be members of WAGGGS or if they were content to remain with the present situation. They were concerned that they were not technically members of the world movement. At that meeting it was agreed that it was important to pursue the matter and keep it a priority. The presence of members at CIGA meetings from the northern diocese was seen as vital in continuing to bring the issue of 'full membership' to the top of the agenda at these meetings.[22]

CGI thought that a way forward might be found through the WAGGGS constitution, but a meeting with Elspeth Henderson, Chair of the Europe Region, confirmed that there was nothing suitable within it to suit the unique CGI situation. She recommended discussions with the Ulster Girl Guiding Association, who represented Northern Ireland through Girlguiding UK at WAGGGS. Due to the sensitive political situation in the North of Ireland, it was recognised that this may require some delicate negotiation. However, discussion with Sue Hogg of the Ulster Guiding Association was amiable and she was very keen to enter into dialogue with CGI, indicative of the trend for cross-community contact. It was clear from this meeting that the Ulster Guiding Association accepted that CGI membership in the North came from a different cultural tradition. It was also appreciated that it was possible for both associations to co-exist and even interact.[23]

On the 8 April 1995 a meeting was arranged between CGI and the Ulster Guiding Association. CGI wanted their support in seeking membership of WAGGGS for their northern members either through CIGA or through some similar body. Sue Hogg listened to suggestions and asked for a copy of CGI's constitution. Subsequently the Ulster Guiding Association proposed that CGI in the North join with them and thus become members of WAGGGS through Girlguiding UK.[24] After careful consideration CGI rejected this:

> The girls were our main consideration, because of the sensitive political to everybody. CGI believes that having the two associations in Northern Ireland for the foreseeable future brings Guiding to all girls whatever their background.[25]

The Good Friday Agreement

CGI were cautious about entering into an arrangement that could prove unworkable. Although peace talks were progressing, communities at the time were very much divided. However, they continued to seek a suitable way for their northern members to become full members of

WAGGGS and negotiations were resumed at a meeting at the World Bureau in London on 22 August 1998. Discussions were difficult but it was eventually agreed to await the implications pertaining to all Guide associations as a result of the implementation of the Good Friday Agreement.[26]

The Good Friday Agreement involved the coming together of all political parties in Northern Ireland to form an executive for government. According to Peter Mandelson, former Secretary of State for Northern Ireland, the new Executive would provide:

> A framework for enhanced practical co-operation across these islands, a framework that allows us to share what we have in common but respects what makes us different. A framework that disperses the rewards of peace through the regions ... I want to see a Northern Ireland with two self-assured traditions but one body of citizens, because it is united by shared language, shared values and shared land, with bonds that are strong enough to encompass diversity of religion, of politics and of custom.[27]

Tensions

It was becoming obvious that tensions and difficulties were being created within the Catholic Guide Association due to the fact that northern members were excluded from many international conferences and seminars. CGI appreciated the difficulties WAGGGS had in upholding the position of political boundaries but they felt that with agreement between all associations involved, it should be possible to allow CGI members north and south to become members of WAGGGS.

1999 WAGGGS World Conference

Through CIGA, CGI and IGG worked together to make preparations for the WAGGGS World Conference held in Dublin in 1999. The issue concerning membership of WAGGGS by northern members was temporarily set aside. The Conference was a massive undertaking for CGI, whose Chief Commissioner at that time was Mary McDonald. The event was held from the 1 to 9 July 1999 at University College Dublin and was the thirtieth WAGGGS World Conference. Guiders from 136 member countries attended, with CIGA acting as hosts. The President of Ireland, Mary McAleese, opened the event and warmly expressed both delight and honour at being invited to welcome delegates to Dublin, particularly those who were visiting for the first time. In her opening address, President McAleese pointed out that:

> While disparities between nations are so obvious in the world of today, Guiding seems to bear witness to the basic goodness in other cultures and instills respect, both for oneself and for others.[28]

At the Conference, Dr Mo Mowlam, then Secretary of State for Northern Ireland, was due to receive the World Citizenship Award for her work in underpinning stability in Northern Ireland. However, continued peace talks kept her from being there to accept the award. At that time the World Citizenship Award, which had been launched by WAGGGS in 1996, had only ever been awarded to two other people: Nelson Mandela and Mary Robinson, then UN High Commissioner for Human Rights and former President of Ireland. The award is given to people outside the Guiding/Scouting movement who have contributed to a better world in the areas of peace, environment, education, food and nutrition, health and culture and heritage. At the conference, Dr Mowlam was described:

> As an example to Girl Guides and Girl Scouts throughout the world of what can be achieved through courage, belief and perseverance. The Secretary of State is herself a Queen's Guide, the highest level of guiding in the UK. Mo Mowlam has acknowledged that many of her successes throughout her life were due to her Guiding training.[29]

The award was accepted on behalf of Dr Mowlam by Helen Jackson MP, Dr Mowlam's Parliamentary Private Secretary.

The delegates at the conference were entertained by a variety of performances. One CGI member recalled:

On Friday night, the delegates were escorted (by the Gardaí) to a performance in the RDS by the young Guides. Being in the audience, I was privy to hear the gasps of excitement and wonder on the part of the delegates as the Guides gave them a taste of our culture and love of music and dance. It was a spectacular event – something which the delegates referred to time and again in the course of the Conference.[30]

Interviews with delegates attending the Conference from around the world highlighted the importance of Guiding. Joyce Angame, of Nagaland, India stated that 'Guiding fulfils a growing need in countries where extra-curricular activities for the young are sadly lacking'. N'Guessan Yaba Angele from the Ivory Coast explained that because 'boys are encouraged to go to school but the girls are kept at home as housekeepers, guiding plays an important educational role'.[31]

Two hundred voluntary leaders played a major role in running the Conference. The younger members of CGI and IGG worked well together throughout the Conference. The 'Service Team' comprised young girls from both associations, all wearing the same uniform and working and cooperating together.

The event received considerable publicity in the media.[32] Messages of thanks were received from many delegations at its conclusion and a tribute was paid in the WAGGGS monthly bulletin, *WAGGGSFACTS*:

> CIGA the Council of Irish Guiding Associations and all their fantastic helpers, did a marvellous job. They

combined so successfully the core of Irish culture with the very best of Irish Guiding and offered it to the World for 8 wonderful days.[33]

Continued Negotiations

CGI continued to seek a solution that did not take into account political boundaries. The Good Friday Agreement allowed the people of Northern Ireland to choose their nationality underpinning their own cultural identity and in this regard CGI hoped that their members in the North would be eligible for membership of WAGGGS through CIGA. However, although CGI claimed to be a thirty-two county association, from a legal perspective, under the terms of the Good Friday Agreement, Articles 2 and 3 of the Irish Constitution of 1937 were amended and all claim to jurisdiction over Northern Ireland had been relinquished. As a consequence there is currently no legally recognised entity comprising the thirty-two counties of Ireland.[34] Therefore CGI northern membership of WAGGGS through CIGA would be unconstitutional.

Following on from the Good Friday Agreement of 1998 it was recognised that an essential aspect of the reconciliation process was to promote a culture of tolerance at every level. Therefore, communication and dialogue across both communities was markedly improved. Against this background CGI asked WAGGGS if would they allow CGI members in the North become full members of WAGGGS through CIGA in the Republic if CGI and the Ulster

Guiding Association worked together to develop Guiding to its fullest potential in the North.[35]

Conclusion

In 2005 the World Bureau appointed a special task group under the chairmanship of Mary Lynn Myers, Deputy Chair of the World Board, to examine the possibilities. In July 2006 they met with the three Chief Commissioners of CGI, IGG and GGUK, and presented them with a recommendation to which a response was required at the World Board meeting in September 2006. They recommended:

> That membership of WAGGGS for CGI members resident in Northern Ireland be provided through affiliation with Girlguiding UK.[36]

They stated that this was the final World Board answer to the question of WAGGGS membership for CGI members in Northern Ireland. The recommendation posed great difficulties for CGI members, with many intense meetings debating the ramifications of the proposal taking place over the following months. The choices were limited to:

- Agreeing to the recommendation
- Retaining the status quo
- Withdrawal from CIGA and from WAGGGS.

After considerable discussion it was agreed that CGI would examine the proposal. An administrative agreement was drawn up between Girlguiding UK and the Catholic Guides of Ireland, 'the purpose of which was to provide membership of WAGGGS for all members of CGI resident in Northern Ireland'.[37]

> This agreement is concluded for administrative reasons only and it is not intended to change the current operation of CGI, either in Northern Ireland or the Republic of Ireland.[38]

The arrangement was still not ideal, with CGI members in the North unable to represent CGI at a world or european conference. The resolution to accept the recommendation caused a lot of heartache for CGI members but the prospect of all girls in CGI becoming members of WAGGGS ultimately influenced the decision.

On 12 April 2008 the National Council voted to accept the proposal issued by WAGGGS as outlined in the administrative arrangement and further accepted the proposed changes to the CIGA Constitution, necessary to facilitate the proposal. This meant that all members of the Catholic Guides of Ireland were members of WAGGGS but only members residing in the Republic of Ireland were members of CIGA.

The current peaceful climate in Northern Ireland has presented all kinds of possibilities for increased dialogue and reaching out between the communities. This was evidenced when Peggy McGoran was chosen as one of a select group of people from across Northern Ireland to be named in the 2009 New Year's Honours List. She will receive an MBE for her voluntary service to the Catholic Guide Movement in the North. She stated:

> I can't stress enough the benefits that come with joining the group for parents and children alike. I think it is a great way for children to spend their teenage years. It's a real social education for all members; it helps to motivate them to try new things and meet new people.[39]

International Charitable Activities

While negotiations progressed concerning membership of WAGGGS at board level, ordinary members of CGI were experiencing the benefits of World Association. McWilliams defines the 1990s as the era of the 'New Irish Dream, where any Irish person can be or have whatever he or she wants. All you have to do is believe in yourself'.[40] He refers to this generation of young people as the 'Expectocracy', a seemingly selfish, self-obsessed grouping whose immediate objective was personal gratification.[41] This generalisation would not apply to members of CGI, whose involvement in charitable causes both at home and abroad continued into the twenty-first century.

In order to further spread the Guiding movement around the world, a voluntary contribution is made annually to the World Association. As can be seen from the views of delegates at the World Conference, Guiding is important for the social and educational development of girls and young women particularly in developing countries. The Thinking Day Fund assists with this development. World Thinking Day falls on the birthday of the founders of Guiding and Scouting, Lord and Lady Baden Powell, 22 February.[42] WAGGGS provide four world centres and each centre offers activities designed to give members of the Guiding movement the opportunity to come together and learn more about other people, cultures and countries. All the centres have a different atmosphere and programme. Catholic Guides in Ireland who participate in international events at these centres are required to report back on their experiences and express how they personally gained, what they learned and how they could apply it to Guiding at home.[43]

In a similar vein, learning about other cultures and countries is the main aim of Overtures, a European network of Guides and Scouts comprising of representatives from over seventeen countries. It is a support group for Guiding and Scouting organisations interested in exploring ways of becoming more open to children of ethnic minorities. As multiculturalism was now an everyday feature of modern society, sharing experiences from other countries can help to identify what works and what doesn't. According to committee member Maria Carroll, 'by participating in the network, both as a participant and at an organisational level, CGI is at the heart of one of the strongest networks in Europe'.[44] To encourage an awareness of other cultures, a weekend was held in Dublin in 2003 titled, 'No Frontiers', the theme of which was anti-racism. Guides from Cork, Dublin and Wexford took part in events that included learning dances, cookery and crafts from around the world.[45]

Whilst creating an awareness of other cultures, CGI was also involved in a range of diverse charitable ventures at an international level. In 2000, as part of the El Salvador Awareness Campaign, CGI members received a grant from the Department of Education for a project titled, 'Open Your Heart and Celebrate Life'. The project encouraged Guides to use a variety of methodologies such as dance, drama, poetry, art and craft, and music to create public awareness of third-world development issues focussing on solidarity, justice and empowerment.

Performances in parish churches were used to inform local communities of the growing debt and plight of those living in the developing world. Over the years, through the Romero Centre in Harold's Cross, Dublin, CGI helped raise funds for food hampers containing a broad range of items including bean and vegetable seeds, tools and bricks for the people of El Salvador and Guatemala who were experiencing unprecedented poverty.[46] Similarly some CGI members were invited to participate in a Global Awareness Project that involved travel to Nigeria, where they actively took part at a community level to raise awareness of HIV and AIDS.[47]

CGI members also took part in seminars on education for girls and young women, with workshops held in Scotland and Denmark aimed at finding methods of education that could reach all members of society. Despite the fact that there indeed existed a culture of self-indulgence in the modern wealthy Ireland of the twenty-first century as articulated by McWilliams, the girls involved in these ventures gave unselfishly of their time.

The Catholic Connection

Although the organisation is no longer involved, from an administrative perspective, with the Catholic church, CGI retains a Catholic connection through involvement with other lay Catholic organisations. The International Catholic Conference of Guiding (ICCG) was recognised in 1965 by the Vatican as an international Guide organisation. Every three years it comes together for a World Conference.

> The mission of ICCG is to help Catholic leaders fulfil their mission of education and service and to help Girl Guides and Girl Scouts to experience more intensely their Christian faith through Guiding. ICCG also aims to bring the Guide movement into the international life of the church and to promote the Catholic aspect of Guiding by developing the Guiding faith on a personal level. In 2000 the aim of the conference was how to meet the spiritual needs of Guides, the role of lay-women in the church and how leaders can be spiritual advisors in a multi-faith society.[48]

The Conference was held for the first time in Africa in answer to an invitation by the Girl Guides of Togo:

This event was important in proving that an African country is just as capable of organising a World Gathering, with the same competences and assets, as an American or European country and in showing that globalisation cannot just be limited to models prevailing in rich countries.[49]

The conference highlighted the gap between rich and poor countries. According to Dolores Farnan who was one of those who attended the conference on behalf of CGI:

The difference a pen and a lollipop can make to a child's life would bring tears to your eyes. This terrible gap between those who have and have not, were some of the thoughts that flashed through our minds. In spite of their circumstances the people are all so full of joy, their smiles, bright eyes, yet they give so much. We have a lot to learn.[50]

Outdoor Pursuits and Milestones

Camping was still a favourite Guide activity and in 1993, Fernhill, the house purchased by the Guides in 1953 for the purposes of camping, celebrated its fortieth birthday. A weekend of fun was organised to celebrate with members past and present gathered for an old fashioned 'camp' including a flag ceremony, campfires and treasure hunts. Over the years the old house in Wicklow had played an important role in the lives of many Guides. The rural retreat provided an escape from the pressures of school and work. Enthusiastically the girls decorated the rooms themselves. They hiked and explored in the beautiful countryside during the day and by night terrified each other with ghost stories around a fire. Friendships were formed and strengthened through team work and companionship. Every year, a week was given over to past members of CGI and their families, providing them with an opportunity to relive their Guiding days. In return they organised fundraising events to help with the upkeep of the house.[51] Tragically, Fernhill was burned to the ground during a recent spate of vandalism.

For the Guides in Cork, 1993 was an historic year, with the opening of their new headquarters in Dominick Street. In Cork, relations between the other Guide and Scout organisations were very good. Outdoor events were organised by the Joint Committee of Scouting and Guiding with adventure days for all. 'Squelch' is one such event and in 1997, five hundred Scouts and Guides took part in what turned out to be a very muddy affair.

The solidarity and friendships between the girls and women created through the organisation were most evident at the seventy-fifth anniversary of the Catholic Guides of Ireland in 2003. A committee was formed to look at ideas for events to mark the occasion. Cecilia Browne was chair of the Committee:

> I was hoping President Mary McAleese could come and say a few words but she was busy on all the dates proposed. I decided to ring up Áras an Uachtaráin and suggest if she couldn't come to us could we go to her. I thought it would be a nice experience for our older members.[52]

Events were organised throughout the year to mark the anniversary with the highlight of the celebrations taking place on Saturday, 27 September 2003. Over 1,400 CGI members arrived in Larch Hill for a 'Fun Day', which was officially launched by Martin King of TV3. The main attraction at the event was Fossett's Circus, which entertained the crowds with two shows. Other forms of entertainment included bouncy castles, face painting and treasure hunts.[53]

The phone call to the Áras paid off and, in January 2004, fifty leaders were invited to meet President Mary McAleese at Áras an Uachtaráin where she spoke to each person individually and thanked them for their services to Guiding.

Shrinking Membership

The new programme, 'Choices', offered a competitive range of activities and courses designed to attract and meet the needs of girls in modern Irish society. However, there was some disquiet at the fall in membership. In an interview with the *Irish Independent*, doubts concerning the future of the Guides was expressed:

> We have waiting lists for girls who want to join the Guides but finding leaders is very hard. We can't get young people to commit themselves. There are a lot of courses that you have to take. Also insurance is another big problem. We're only allowed a certain ratio of girls to leaders.[54]

It is generally accepted by members within CGI that considerable effort was put into having the organisation recognised by the World Association and that this was to the detriment of the development of the organisation. A marked drop in membership was considered to be as a result of many factors. As the article above points out, government child safety regulations stipulate that there must be a certain ratio of children to a responsible carer. This has placed pressure on the organisation to seek an increased number of suitable committed leaders, while waiting lists of children wanting to join are growing. Other factors such as playstations, computer games and exams, along with the wide variety of activities on offer for girls to choose from that compete with Guide activities, were considered responsible for the drop in membership.

Despite efforts to update the image of the organisation in the early 1990s, an old-fashioned perception remained. This presented as a consistent reason for rejection by older girls when trying to recruit for leaders. A survey of second-level students between the ages of 14 and 19 was carried out in 2008/9 and revealed that there was little awareness of the organisation as a whole. In many cases those surveyed articulated an Americanised version of Guiding based around selling cookies. Other negative features identified were the uniform, which was still associated with being brown in colour, the fact that the Guides was a single-sex organisation and, for some, that it was associated with the Catholic church: all these added to the overall old-fashioned image. The survey made a comparison between the activities offered in the Guide programme and outside of it. The second-level students were asked what activities they were currently involved in and amongst those listed were drama, dancing, singing, public speaking, sports and outdoor activities. It is interesting to note that all of these activities are included in the Guide programme.

Management Issues

In 1994 it was acknowledged at a National Executive Board meeting that internal structural problems too were hampering efficient management.[55] It is generally agreed by all members at Board level that the organisation still tends to function along the old, pre-1977 diocesan structure. This creates problems for effective management as a National Association:

> Policies are there but whether people implement them or not is another thing. You have to bring people along with you and work together, that's a big problem in our association and very frustrating. I think as an association we need to stand back and look at ourselves.[56]

There are various areas within the organisation currently being examined to ascertain ways of improving communication and efficiency. In the North, the Northern Region Committee was set up in 1992 to promote and develop Guiding and to administer grant aid to the five northern dioceses of the Catholic Guides of Ireland. The committee employed a full-time development officer and a part-time secretary. The new administrative arrangement required a new office and in March 1993 a suitable premises was found.[57] Currently, as an experimental test case, the northern Guides are attempting to implement a new scheme which will divide the diocese in the North into areas. It is hoped that these areas will become much more streamlined and manageable and that as a consequence, communication between local companies and the area managers will be enhanced. On the success of this management restructure it is hoped to have the scheme adopted by CGI in the rest of the country.

The Catholic Guides of Ireland have reached an important stage in the development of their organisation. An acknowledgement of the problems hampering development has galvanised the National and Executive Boards to address the issues. The Catholic Guides of Ireland have survived disputes, wars, economic upturns and downturns, and social upheaval; therefore, it is unlikely they will face any problems they cannot surmount. A dynamic powerful group of women have come together to deal with the findings of the survey outlined above and to improve communications within the organisation. Considerable energy and debate has triggered a focussed approach at board level and this has improved dialogue overall.

The Future

At the time of writing a fresh, out-going, achievable plan of action has begun to generate new membership. This, together with other factors such as the slump in the economy, has led to a re-evaluation of what is important to young people. A less materialistic, competitive lifestyle has created a desire for a more ethical, caring, community-based society. As stated in the Guiders Handbook, Guiding provides girls and young women with an opportunity to learn how to set goals, solve problems and reach conclusions. They learn to move steadily, and with increasing confidence, away from the dependency of early childhood towards the interdependent relationships that characterise successful maturity.[58]

Through Guiding, girls learn to share common values and to experience the value of friendship between each other and Guides of other cultures throughout the world. They learn to work collaboratively and co-operatively in non-competitive settings. Guides practise everyday living skills from public speaking to basic first aid, with personal character building as part of the process. They are encouraged to do their best, to collaborate rather than compete, to build on successes, to expand into extra curricular activities, to develop personal skills, to link with the outside world through community activity and helpfulness, and to develop team spirit through work with peers.[59] In short, Guiding is preparation for life.

Nineteen hundred and twenty eight – a year to remember for sure
We opened our doors to girls of all ages – didn't matter if rich or if
poor
We offered them friendships, challenges and camping, new skills,
fun and laughter and more
We asked in return for their promise, commitment and loyalty to
the values we bore
Two thousand and eight – the year has just passed – eighty years
have already gone by
Our doors are still opened around this green isle and the memories
we have are piled high
We've changed how we look to the world looking on, we're as
bright as the sun in the sky
But the values we cherish, the promise we make, and the
friendships – they'll never die!
We're proud of our past – we won't let it go and our future is still
in the making
What we offer today is the same as the past, it's just in more
modern packaging
The friendship, the fun, the challenges, the skills, the laughter all
there for the taking
Have you time on your hands, have you got what it takes? If so,
go on then – come Guiding!

Carol Ewings
Chief Commissioner
2005–2009

Notes

1. US President Bill Clinton, Address to the joint session of the Houses of the Oíreachtas, Dáil Éireann, 1 December 1995
2. David McWilliams, *The Pope's Children: Ireland's New Elite* (Dublin, 2006) p. 30–31
3. *Irish Independent*, Friday, 18 December 1992
4. Ibid.
5. Ibid.
6. Caroline Kennedy, Public Relations & Marketing, brief on new logo, 11 September 1992, Sheila Redmond collection
7. Ibid.
8. Marketing Development Programme, the Michael Smurfit Graduate School of Business, Blackrock, Co. Dublin, CGI Survey 1999, p. 89
9. UCD Marketing Development Programme, the Michael Smurfit Graduate School of Business, Blackrock, Co. Dublin
10. Interview with Josephine Higgins, Belfast, 21 February 2009
11. Targets and Strategies for 2000, Annual Report 2000, Clanwilliam Terrace
12. *Irish Independent*, Monday, 20 February 2006
13. Diarmaid Ferriter, *The Transformation of Ireland, 1900–2000* (London, 2005) p. 740–43
14. Ibid.
15. National Youth Health Programme Report of the National Task Force on Obesity, 2004, Electronic Sources
16. Guiders Handbook, CGI, Clanwilliam Terrace
17. In conversation with Cork CGI members, 10 March 2009; in conversation with Belfast CGI members, 21 February 2009
18. In conversation with Cecilia Browne, National Treasurer, CGI, 6 May 2009
19. Diarmaid Ferriter, *The Transformation of Ireland: 1900–2000* (London, 2005) p. 734–39
20. Child Protection Policy, CGI Clanwilliam Terrace, 1998
21. CGI Handbook for Guiders, Clanwilliam Terrace
22. Minutes of National Executive Board Meeting, 1994–1996, Clanwilliam Terrace

23. Synopsis of Achievement of the Aims of CIGA, CIGA files, Clanwilliam Terrace
24. Minutes of National Executive Board Meeting, 1994–1996, Clanwilliam Terrace
25. Synopsis of Achievement of the Aims of CIGA, CIGA files, Clanwilliam Terrace
26. Ibid.
27. Peter Mandelson, 'The Good Friday Agreement: A Vision for a New Order in Northern Ireland', in Marianne Elliott, *The Long Road to Peace in Northern Ireland* (Cambridge, 2002) pp. 116–17
28. President Mary McAleese, opening address, World Conference newsletter, Clanwilliam Terrace
29. World Citizenship Award, World Conference newsletter, Clanwilliam Terrace
30. Guiders Link, September/October 1999 – Sheila Redmond Collection.
31. Interviews with delegates, World Conference newsletter, Clanwilliam Terrace
32. Ibid.
33. Guiders Link, September/October 1999
34. Frank Keane Solicitors, in response to queries from Dolores Farnan, CIGA file, Mairead Quinn collection, Clanwilliam Terrace
35. Minutes of CIGA meeting, 20 November 2005, Clanwilliam Terrace
36. Confidential document for circulation to NEB members, July 2006, Mairead Quinn, CIGA file, Clanwilliam Terrace
37. Confidential briefing document, August 2006, Betty O'Donovan collection, Clanwilliam Terrace
38. Agreement of Association between Girlguiding UK and Catholic Guides of Ireland, Mairead Quinn, CIGA file, Clanwilliam Terrace
39. Article re. Peggy McGoran, *Mourne Observer*, 7 January 2009
40. David McWilliams, *The Pope's Children* (Dublin, 2006) p. 53
41. Ibid., p. 54

42. Thinking Day, Catholic Guides of Ireland International Handbook, Clanwilliam Terrace
43. International Events, Catholic Guides of Ireland International Handbook, Clanwilliam Terrace
44. Catholic Guides of Ireland, Annual Report 2006, Overtures Steering Committee, Clanwilliam Terrace
45. Catholic Guides of Ireland, Annual Report, 2003
46. Guiders Link 2007
47. Ibid.
48. Catholic Guides of Ireland, Annual Report 2006, ICCG Report, Clanwilliam Terrace
49. ICCG, Catholic Guides of Ireland Annual Report 2000, Clanwilliam Terrace
50. ICCG, Dolores Farnan, Catholic Guides of Ireland Annual Report 2000, Clanwilliam Terrace
51. In conversation with Cecilia Browne, National Treasurer, 6 May 2009
52. In conversation with Cecilia Browne, National Treasurer, CGI
53. Catholic Guides of Ireland, Annual Report, 2003
54. *Irish Independent*, 5 January 2004
55. Minutes of National Executive Board meeting, April 1994
56. Interview with Josephine Higgins, Belfast, 21 February 2009
57. Annual Report 1993, Catholic Guides of Ireland, Clanwilliam Terrace
58. Guiders Handbook, CGI, Clanwilliam Terrace, p. 8
59. Ibid., p. 9

CONCLUSION

Research for this book has unveiled the commitment of an extraordinary group of women who, on a voluntary basis, devote their time to developing a youth movement for girls based on the principles of Guiding. It became compelling, as interviews with members progressed, to understand what could be driving their commitment. They used words such as 'challenges', 'life skills', 'confidence', 'discipline', 'teamwork' and, the most common, 'friendship'. Interviews with retired members were similar but revealed stories of girls and young women living in a different Ireland, facing challenges in a country gripped by wartime rationing, economic hardships, religious fervour, increasing liberalisation and political divisions. They talked about the different skills they had acquired through Guiding to help them get by, and about the friendships they had formed that saw them through the hard times. These were the stories of no ordinary women.

To begin my research, I invited a group of ex-Guides from Waterford to attend a get-together in the Tower Hotel to share their memories of Guiding. The women varied in age and many of them had not seen each other since they were children. As they walked into the room the first signs of recognition led to cries of 'I haven't seen you in ages', 'You haven't changed a bit' and 'What on earth did you do to your hair'! After they exchanged warm greetings the women began to reminisce about their days in the Guides. They recalled stories of hikes, camps and outings to the beach. They remembered too the old Guide songs and with a little encouragement they started to sing. They sang a number of songs and there was even a little bit of harmony. There was also something extremely poignant in the fact that they could remember every single word of all the Guide songs they sang as children.

There were similar experiences in Cork, Belfast and Dublin, where past and present members recalled personal memories of Guiding and what their experiences had meant to them. One woman believed that she would not have progressed so far in her career had she not been encouraged as a Guide to stand up and speak in front of an audience for her public speaking badge. Another member expressed the tremendous gratitude she felt to the Guides who bestowed so much comfort on her when her mother died while she was very young. For her, the Guides had become a family. Another member still laughs as she recalls how she and three others pitched a tent on a hillside; then, after falling asleep exhausted after a day of hiking they woke in a heap at the bottom of the hill having slid a considerable distance while still asleep.

For members in the North the troubles were a constant challenge to Guiding, but this did not deter them. Women who were Guides at the height of the unrest believe that Guiding provided stability and reassurance.

All members talk of the friends they have made. One woman vividly recalled how she and a group of friends sat out under the stars discussing the meaning of life until the sun came up. These women are linked by a common bond; even if they haven't met for many years, they can instantly rekindle their childhood memories and resume their friendships as if they had seen each other only yesterday. The saying must be true then, once a Guide always a Guide.

The story of the Catholic Guides of Ireland is the story of a success. A voluntary, charitable organisation, it continues to do what it set out to do in 1928 and improve the lives of girls and young women through Guiding. The women volunteers who manage CGI are devoted to the organisation's mission and play a major role in the execution of a range of activities vital for its survival. Thus, a wide variety of creative and adventurous pursuits are offered to girls in an open, friendly environment. The magic of Guiding prevails and in the Catholic Guides of Ireland the spirit of adventure is indomitable.

APPENDIX

National Officers Since 1977

Chief Commissioners

Maureen Sloan	1977–1982
Bridie Dolan	1982–1988
Dolores Farnan	1988–1992
Betty O'Donovan	1992–1997
Mary McDonald	1997–2001
Máire McGrath	2001–2005
Carol Ewings	2005–2009
Catherine Lenihan	2009

Assistant Chief Commissioners

Cecilia Browne	1999–2006
Dolores Farnan	2006

National Secretary

Rita Daly	1977–1983
Darina Lynch	1983–1986
Siobhan Corry	1986–1991
Mary McDonald	1992–1997
Lorraine Coakley	1997–1998
Betty O'Donovan	1998–2003
Martha McGrath	2003–2007
Martha McGrath	2008

National Treasurer

Betty Monaghan	1977–1983
Rita Daly	1983–1989
Betty O'Donovan	1989–1992
Eileen Murphy	1992–1998
Máire McGrath	1998–2001
Anne Quinlan	2001–2003
Cecilia Browne	2006

Sources

Collections

Betty O'Donovan collection, Memories of Early Days of the Catholic Girl Guides of Ireland, by Sr M. Magdalen, Missionaries of Mary

Betty O'Donovan collection, Guide Memories of Camp in Cork

Betty O'Donovan collection, How It All Began, leaflet

Betty O'Donovan collection, letters, diary, memorabilia of Betty Casey

Betty O'Donovan collection, scrapbook, newspaper articles

Betty O'Donovan collection, letter to M. O'Kennedy re. Federation 6 April 1971

Maureen Walsh née Loftus collection, letter dated 22 November 1934

May McGrath collection, Diary

May McGrath collection, logbook Buidean Eidín

May McGrath collection, minute book

Sheila Redmond collection, merit badge book (1978)

Sheila Redmond collection, letter 4 February 1975

Paula Brackenbury collection, logbook

Maureen Sloan collection, Joint Guide/Scout Knock Committee

Maureen Sloan collection, Papal Visit

Mairead Quinn collection, CIGA files

Appendix

Interviews

Maureen Walsh née Loftus, Greystones, Co. Wicklow, 4 May 2009

May McGrath, Ballyfermot, 8 September 2008

May Garvan, Rathgar, Dublin, 16 September 2008

Betty O'Donovan, Clanwilliam Terrace, 21 August 2008

Sheila Redmond, Cabra, 9 September 2008

Pat Walsh, Churchtown, 3 October 2008

Carmel Hutchin, Fairview, 6 September 2008

Marian Stewart and Máire McGrath, Belfast Office, 6 October 2008

Josephine Higgins, Belfast, 21 February 2009

Group Interview, Waterford, 20 November 2008

Group Interview, Belfast 21 February 2009

Group Interview, Cork, 10 March 2009

Cecilia Browne, 6 May 2009

Sean Loftus, 10 May 2009

May Dowling and Antoinette Long, Cork, 9 March 2009

Fr A. J. Gaughan, Blackrock, 7 September 2008

Fr Jim O'Sullivan, Balllinteer, 30 September 2008

Other Sources

Dublin Diocesan Archives (papers of Archbishop Edward Byrne), AB8/6/XXI/18

Harrington Street Archive, HSA 1–6

UCD Special Collections Dept, James Joyce Library,

Constitution of the Catholic Girl Guides, 1936

Lennon, Peter, *The Rocky Road to Dublin* (1968)

Documentary on Irish Life in the 1960s

At Home With the Clearys, Documentary, RTÉ 1, screened 3 September 2007, 9.30 p.m.
CGI Survey, Marketing Development Programme, the Michael Smurfit Graduate School of Business (1999)
CGI Survey Clare Brophy 2008/9

Newspapers

Cork Examiner, June 1932
Irish Independent, July 1932
Cork Examiner, April 1934
Irish Press, July 1953
Dublin Evening Mail, November 1954
Irish Independent, April 1955
Irish Independent, May 1955
Irish Press, July 1956
Dublin Evening Mail, March 1957
Irish Press, July 1957
Evening Press, March 1958
Irish Press, July 1958
Cork Examiner, May 1960
Sunday Independent, November 1963
The Irish Times, September 1966
Evening Herald, July 1973
Cork Examiner, April 1977
Evening Press, September 1979
The Irish Times, September 1979
Irish Independent, June 1980
Irish Independent, May 1981
Evening Herald, July 1990

Evening Echo, July 1991
Irish Independent, December 1992
Irish Independent, January 2004
Irish Independent, February 2006
Irish Independent, September 2007
Mourne Observer, January 2009

Contemporary Books and Articles 1928–2009
The Italian Youth of Catholic Action, leaflet (undated)
HSA3
The Aspirant Tests (1945), CGI Archive, Clanwilliam
Terrace
The Catholic Girl Guide (1941)
The Second Class Tests (1945)
Irish Catholic (1940)
An banóglac (1955)
Wexford, 50th Anniversary Booklet
Forde Walter, 'The Aimless Rebellion', in *Christus Rex*,
Vol., XXI, number 1, January 1967
Thornley, David, 'Ireland: End of an Era?' in *Studies*, Vol.
53, 1–17, spring 1964, p. 16
Merit Badge Book (1978)
Guiders Link 1982
Guiders Link 1983
Holy Trinity Guides, *40th Anniversary Booklet 1965–2005*
Trimby A., *Collection of Poems on the Theme of Peace*
compiled by the Catholic Guides of Ireland
Cozens-Hardy, Beryl, T*he Essential Elements of
Girl/Guiding/Girl Scouting* (London, 1975/82)

Memories of Guiding, St Paul's Girl Guide Unit, 1967–2007 (Belfast)
CGI Guiders Handbook
Guiders Link 1987/88
Guiders Link 1989/90
World Conference Newsletter (1999)
Guiders Link 1999
Catholic Guides of Ireland International Handbook
Catholic Guides of Ireland Annual Report 1993/2000/2003/2006
Guiders Link 2007

Government Documents

Dáil Debates, Vol. 42, 2 June 1932, Mr Derrig Minister for Education
Dáil Debates, Vol. 77, 27 September 1939, Mr Aiken Minister for Defence
Government Commissioned Report (William Norton) Causes and consequences of the present level and trend in population, 5 April 1954, Official Documents Department, UCD

Electronic Sources

The Birch Bark Roll, Histoclo.com/youth/c1900.htm
National Youth Health Programme Report of the National Task Force on Obesity (2004)
www.youthhealth.ie
Wintergarden and Theatre Royal Complex, arthurlloyd.co.uk
www.scouts.ie

BIBLIOGRAPHY

Arthur, Paul Conflict, 'Memory and Reconciliation' in *The Long Road to Peace in Northern Ireland* (ed.) Marianne Elliott (Cambridge, 2002)

Boylan, Henry, *Dictionary of Irish Biography* (Dublin, 1999)

Browne, Terence, *Ireland: A Social and Cultural History 1922–2002* (London, 2004)

Clear, Caitriona, *Women of the House: Women's Household Work in Ireland, 1922–1961* (Dublin, 2000)

Coogan, Tim Pat, *Disillusioned Decades: Ireland 1966–1987* (Dublin, 1987)

Cooney, John, *John Charles McQuaid* (Dublin, 1994)

Coote, A. & Campbell, B., *Sweet Freedom: The Struggle for Women's Liberation* (London, 1982)

D'Arcy, Brian, *A Different Journey* (Dublin, 2006)

Doyle, Paul A., *Paul Vincent Carroll* (New York, 1971)

Fallon, Brian, *An Age of Innocence: Irish Culture 1930–1960* (Dublin, 1998)

Fanning, Ronan, *Independent Ireland* (Dublin, 1983)

Ferriter, Diarmaid, *The Transformation of Ireland 1900–2000* (London, 2005)

Foster, R.F., *Modern Ireland: 1600–1972* (London, 1989)

Gaughan, A.J. *Scouting in Ireland* (Dublin, 2006)

Gray, Tony, *Ireland this Century* (London, 1994)

Hennessy, Thomas, *Northern Ireland: The Origins of the Troubles* (Dublin, 2005)

Hill, Myrtle, *Women in Ireland: A Century of Change* (Belfast, 2003)

Jackson, Alvin, *Ireland 1798–1998* (London, 2003)

Keogh, Dermot, *Twentieth Century Ireland: Nation and State* (Dublin, 1994)

Keogh, Dermot, 'Church, State and Society' in *De Valera's Constitution and Ours* (ed.) Brian Farrell (Dublin, 1988)

Kilfeather, Siobhan, 'Irish Feminism' in *The Cambridge Companion to Modern Irish Culture* (eds) Joe Cleary and Claire Connolly (Cambridge, 2005)

Levine, June, *Sisters: The Personal Story of an Irish Feminist* (Dublin, 1982)

McAvoy, Sandra L., 'The Regulation of Sexuality in the Irish Free State 1929–1935' in *Medicine, Disease and the State in Ireland 1650–1940*, (eds) Greta Jones and Elizabeth Malcolm (Cork, 1999)

McWilliams, David, *The Pope's Children: Ireland's New Elite* (Dublin, 2006)

Mandelson, Peter, 'The Good Friday Agreement: A Vision for a New Order in Northern Ireland' in *The Long Road to Peace in Northern Ireland* (ed.) Marianne Elliott (Cambridge, 2002)

Marwick, Arthur, *The Sixties: Cultural Revolution in Britain, France, Italy and the United States* (Oxford, 1998)

Mullarkey, Kieran, 'Ireland, the Pope and Vocationalism: The Impact of the Encyclical *Quadragesimo Anno*' in *Ireland in the 1930s*, Joost Augustejn (Dublin, 1999)

Murray, Patrick, *Oracles of God: The Roman Catholic Church and Irish Politics* (Dublin, 2000)

Peukert, Detlev, *The Weimar Republic: The Crisis of Classical Modernity* (New York, 1993)

Robinson, Mary, in Helen Exley, *In Celebration of Women: A Selection of Words and Paintings* (London, 1996)

Stachura, P., *The German Youth Movement 1900–1945* (London, 1981)

Valiulis, Gianella Maryann & O'Dowd Mary (eds) *Women & Irish History: Essays in honour of Margaret MacCurtain* (Dublin 1997)

Whyte, J.H., *Church and State in Modern Ireland, 1923–1979* (Dublin 1984)

Wills, Clair, *That Neutral Island: A Cultural History of Ireland During the Second World War* (London, 2007)

INDEX